food combining

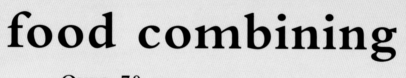

food combining

OVER 70 FAST AND DELICIOUS RECIPES BASED ON THE SIMPLE AND HEALTHY HAY DIET

GILLY LOVE AND
PATRIZIA DIEMLING

LORENZ BOOKS

Lorenz Books is an imprint of
Anness Publishing Limited
Hermes House
88–89 Blackfriars Road
London SE1 8HA

www.lorenzbooks.com

This edition distributed in Canada by Raincoast Books
9050 Shaughnessy Street, Vancouver, BC, V6P 6E5

Publisher Joanna Lorenz
Senior Cookery Editor Linda Fraser
Copy Editor Christine Ingram
Indexer Hilary Bird
Designer Ian Sandom
Photography Thomas Odulate
Food for Photography Patrizia Diemling, assisted by Mary McCabe
Styling Gilly Love
Illustrator Madeleine David
Cover Design DW Design
Production Controller Don Campaniello

Previously published as Healthy Eating Library Series: *The Food Combining Cookbook*

Printed and bound in China

© Anness Publishing Limited 1997 1999
Updated © 2001

3 5 7 9 10 8 6 4 2

NOTES

For all recipes, quantities are given in both metric and imperial measures and,
where appropriate, measures are also given in standard cups and spoons.
Follow one set, but not a mixture, because they are not interchangeable.

Standard spoon and cup measures are level.
1 tsp = 5ml, 1 tbsp = 15ml, 1 cup = 250ml/8fl oz

Australian standard tablespoons are 20ml. Australian readers should use 3 tsp
in place of 1 tbsp for measuring small quantities of gelatine, cornflour, salt, etc.

Medium eggs are used unless otherwise stated.

CONTENTS

Introduction 6

Starters and Soups 10

Meat and Poultry 22

Fish and Seafood 32

Vegetables and Salads 44

Grains, Pulses and Rice 56

Pasta and Pastry 66

Cakes, Bakes and Biscuits 76

Desserts 86

Index 96

INTRODUCTION

Some 80 years ago, an American doctor, Dr William Howard Hay, developed an entirely new system of eating. He had found that a person's health and well-being were largely determined by what they ate. Dr Hay had suffered from a debilitating kidney disease, but by experimenting with his diet he was able to alleviate the symptoms dramatically.

Over the years since Dr Hay first developed his theories, thousands of people have found that following the Hay System has improved their health, increased their levels of energy and enabled them to maintain an optimum body weight. Scientific research also points to the fact that a diet that includes plenty of fresh fruit and raw vegetables every day can reduce the chance of developing such conditions as heart disease, strokes and many cancers.

THE HAY SYSTEM

The principles of the Hay system of eating were remarkably simple and they have changed little over the years. Aware that the body contains alkaline and acid mineral salts in a proportion of 4 to 1, Dr Hay concluded that this balance should be maintained by eating foods with corresponding amounts of alkaline and acid salts. Fruit, most vegetables and herbs are alkaline-forming foods. The Hay system of eating is largely about increasing the consumption of these foods so that our diet mimics the balance in the body.

Hay also found that proteins and carbohydrates, though both acid-forming, need different conditions for digestion and should never be eaten at the same meal. Food combining means using these principles to classify foods and combine compatible foods to provide three basic types of meals – protein, neutral and starch.

FOOD CLASSIFICATION

Food is basically classified as follows:

Alkaline-forming foods: all fresh fruits and green and root vegetables (except starchy vegetables). The Hay diet recommends that we should eat four portions of these foods for every one portion of acid-forming foods. The alkaline- or acid-forming nature of a food has nothing to do with the flavour – some acid-tasting foods, like citrus fruits, are good sources of alkaline salts.

Concentrated proteins (acid-forming foods): meat, poultry, game, fish, eggs and cheese.

Concentrated carbohydrates (acid-forming): grains, flours, bread, pasta, rice and all sugars.

Below, clockwise from top: Apples, apricots, passion fruits, dates, oranges, strawberries, raspberries, pears, blueberries and blackberries, are all alkaline-forming.

Above: Concentrated protein foods, which are all acid-forming foods, include (clockwise from top) milk, eggs, meat, fish and shellfish, as well as poultry and game.

Dr Hay's Basic Principles

• Never mix concentrated carbohydrates and concentrated proteins. Although both are acid-forming, they are not compatible. Proteins require an acid environment in the digestive tract, while to digest starch most efficiently the body needs an alkaline medium. If the two are mixed, the acid medium is partly neutralized and proteins are then only partly digested.

• Leave 4–5 hours between a starch and a protein meal.

• Make fresh fruits and vegetables form the major part of your daily eating. Try to eat three or four portions of fruit, vegetables or salad every day. Ideally they should be raw, or in case of the vegetables, lightly steamed or stir-fried.

• Avoid all processed and refined foods. This is another important rule, although quite hard to follow as so much of our food – canned beans, biscuits, cakes, ready-made meals and so on – comes in processed form. Get into the habit of making your own home-made cakes and biscuits and, whenever possible, use whole grains rather than the refined white alternative, be it pasta, rice, bread or flour.

The following table gives a quick reference to which foods are compatible. It divides foods into three separate food groups: protein, neutral and starch. The neutral foods may be combined with *either* protein foods *or* starch foods. The important rule is *never* to mix protein foods and starch foods in the same meal.

Protein Foods	Neutral Foods	Starch Foods
Meat	Butter	All cereals - wheat, barley, millet, maize, oats and rye
Poultry	Cream and crème fraîche	
Game	Cream cheese	Bread
Fish and shellfish	Egg yolks	Flour
Whole eggs	Olive oil, sunflower oil, sesame oil and walnut oil	Oatmeal
Cheese		Very sweet fruits – bananas, very ripe pears, papaya, very sweet grapes, figs, dates and dried fruits
Milk and yogurt★	All nuts, except peanuts	
	Nut and seed butters, except peanut butter	
All fruits except very sweet fruits (*see* Starch Foods)	All green and root vegetables, except starchy vegetables (*see* Starch Foods)	Pulses and beans, except soya beans
Soya beans and tofu		Peanuts and peanut butter
Cooked tomatoes	All salads and sprouted beans and seeds	Starchy vegetables – potatoes, yams, sweet potatoes, sweetcorn and Jerusalem artichokes
Lemon tea		
Grape juice, the less sweet varieties	All herbs and spices	Sweet grape juice
	Honey and maple syrup	
Tomato juice, canned and vacuum-packed	Water	Beer, lager and stout
		Sweet wines and liqueurs
Dry wines and dry cider	Herb teas	
	Tomato juice, fresh	
★Milk and yogurt are classified as protein foods, but a little of either can be combined with starch	All vegetable juices	
	Yeast-extract drinks	
	Gin and most spirits	
	Weak coffee or tea in moderation	

Note that this table should be used for checking the compatibility of foods. It is not concerned with whether foods are alkaline- or acid-forming.

Can I Do It?

Although at first glance, a food combining diet seems complicated and prescriptive, you will find in a surprisingly short time how easy and enjoyable it is. It is important not to think in terms of "giving up" all those mixed meals, like cheese sandwiches and fish and chip suppers. Instead concentrate on the positive side. Sandwiches made with wholemeal bread or pittas and stuffed with salad can be equally delicious. Or try Roasted Cod with Fresh Tomato Sauce served with a generous portion of Baked Vegetable Chips. Many people who follow this system of eating are delighted to find that they gradually lose excess pounds, without ever once feeling hungry. In addition, all the meals contained in this book are suitable for family eating, so if your principal intention for following the system is to lose weight, you will not feel isolated, but can continue enjoying meals with family and friends. The recipes in this book are simple and relatively quick to prepare and cook. As well as many tasty suggestions for family eating, there are also recipes for more sophisticated meals, from luncheons to dinner parties. The occasional treat is not excluded either and there are delicious desserts to combine with both protein and starch main courses, as well as a choice of home-made breads and cakes.

Using this Book

Each recipe is labelled individually with a "P" to indicate a protein dish or an "S" to show a starch dish. "N" means the dish is neutral, which indicates it can be combined with either a protein or a starch meal. If, for instance, you wished to serve Lentil Risotto with Vegetables (S), you could first serve Gazpacho Salsa (N). This salsa could also be served with Salmon with Yogurt and Mint Dressing (P). Try to balance your daily menu, so that you have one starch, one protein and one neutral dish a day.

INGREDIENTS

Above: Vegetables that are neutral include (clockwise from top): salad leaves, cabbage, fennel, tomatoes, mushrooms, carrots, turnips, parsnips and spring onions.

FRUITS

It would be difficult to overstate the importance of fresh fruit in a healthy diet. Recent studies in the UK and the USA have testified to its protective role as regards health. Try to eat at least two pieces of preferably raw fruit each day. Ideally, it should be eaten on an empty stomach, since the digestion of fruit is much faster when eaten on its own. Alternatively, leave 15 minutes between courses, so that fruit can digest partly by itself. This is particularly important with melon, which does not digest well with other food.

Fruit is an excellent way to start the day as the natural sugars give instant energy. Most fruits can precede or follow a protein course. For starch meals, choose very sweet fruits, like ripe bananas, papayas or pears. Dried fruits – such as dates, sultanas, raisins and figs – are also better combined with starch meals.

Always be sure to choose fruit in peak condition and, if possible, buy the organic variety. Lemons, especially if you are using the rind for flavouring or dressing, should be unwaxed.

VEGETABLES AND SALADS

Vegetables and salads are also enormously important in a food combining diet. All green and root vegetables, together with salads and herbs, are deemed neutral, which means they can be combined with either protein or starch foods. The exceptions are vegetables like potatoes, sweet potatoes, Jerusalem artichokes, sweetcorn and yams, which have a high starch content and are not compatible with protein meals. Tomatoes, on the other hand, though neutral when raw, become very acid once cooked and should be combined only with protein dishes.

Always make sure vegetables are absolutely fresh and, preferably, organic. Although these are likely to cost a little more, vegetables are so central to a food combining diet that you will find it worth spending extra in this area since you will need to buy less in the way of meat, poultry and fish. Vegetables and salads will become the centrepiece of a meal, while proteins and carbohydrates, though still important in dietary terms, will feature less and be served almost as the accompaniment.

Above: Neutral foods include (clockwise from top) fresh herbs, peppercorns, yeast extract, garlic, fresh ginger, maple syrup and and chilli sauce.

HERBS AND SPICES

Fresh herbs are indispensable ingredients in a food combining diet. Being neutral, like vegetables, they can be used with either protein or starch meals, where they not only add their own flavour but bring intrinsic nutritional benefit too. Many, like mint and bay, aid digestion, while parsley and chervil are rich in Vitamins A and C. Use fresh herbs whenever possible, for flavour and nutritional value. Many herbs can be grown in the garden or in pots on the kitchen window sill, and this is the best way to ensure you have a constant and ever-fresh supply.

Similarly, spices should also be as fresh as possible, so buy small quantities of the whole seeds and grind in a coffee grinder or spice mill. Black pepper should be freshly ground to ensure freshness and always use sea salt, preferably grinding this too in a salt mill.

Above, clockwise from top: Sprouted mung beans, kidney beans, lentils, tofu, sunflower seeds and mung beans (centre) are all good sources of protein.

PROTEIN FOODS

Protein is essential in a healthy diet but we need only small quantities. Meat and fish, together with eggs and dairy products, are the best sources of protein. If possible, buy organic meat and free-range chicken. Eggs should always be free-range. Grains, pulses and nuts are also good sources of protein and should be a regular part of a vegetarian diet. Sprouted seeds and pulses contain living enzymes that help promote good digestion, tissue growth and repair. Unlike many dried pulses, which are frequently hard to digest, sprouted seeds and pulses are easily digested and are compatible with both protein and starch meals.

SWEETENERS

Refined sugar should be avoided as far as is reasonably possible. Honey, maple syrup or sweet fruits like dates, figs and raisins can be used to sweeten desserts.

SPROUTING BEANS, SEEDS AND PULSES

Green and brown lentils; dried mung, aduki, haricot, flageolet and soya beans; whole dried peas, chick-peas and seeds, such as sunflower and pumpkin, will sprout successfully. Purpose-made sprouters are available from health food stores. If there is no visible sign of germination after about 48 hours, the beans are likely to be old and will never grow.

To sprout beans, seeds and pulses, place 45ml/3 tbsp beans, seeds or pulses in a large, wide-mouthed jar and cover with 250ml/8fl oz/1 cup fresh tepid water. Cover the jar with muslin, secure with an elastic band and leave overnight. Remove the cover and rinse the beans thoroughly with fresh tepid water. Drain well, replace the cover and turn the jar on its side, spacing out the beans, seeds or pulses. Keep the jar in a warm room, out of direct sunlight. Rinse the beans, seeds or pulses daily through the muslin top. The sprouts are ready to eat when there is about 1cm/½in of shoot showing. Rinse and drain thoroughly, then store for up to 2 days in a plastic bag in the fridge.

Above: Wholegrain foods, such as wholemeal flour and bread, brown rice, wild rice and oats are concentrated carbohydrates.

STARCH FOODS

Starches are concentrated carbohydrates, they are an essential part of our diet, providing energy for the body. The best starches are found in wholegrains. Choose wholemeal bread, flour and pasta, and brown rice in preference to white. For special occasions, a little white flour does no harm, providing your diet contains plenty of the fibre found in fruit and vegetables.

FATS AND OILS

All fats and oils, including butter, egg yolks, olive oil, sunflower oil, cream cheese, cream and crème fraîche, are neutral foods and can be combined with either protein or starch meals. Avoid margarines and low-fat spreads as they are highly processed.

Above, clockwise from top: Olive oil, egg yolk, butter, cream cheese and cream are neutral foods.

Some fat is essential in a healthy diet, but most experts agree that we eat far more than is required. A food combining diet is generally low in fat, especially as it eliminates the hidden fats found in biscuits and cakes.

FRESH STOCKS

Fish and vegetable stock are used extensively in the recipes in this book, and while there are some excellent stock cubes and vegetable bouillon powders available, nothing quite matches the flavour of home-made stock. Both can be frozen successfully, but are best if freshly made.

FISH STOCK (P)

To make about 1.2 litres/2 pints/ 5 cups fish stock, thoroughly wash 675g/1½lb white fish bones and trimmings. Melt 15g/½oz/1 tbsp butter in a large, heavy-based saucepan and fry 25g/1oz chopped onion, 25g/1oz chopped leek (white part only) and 25g/1oz chopped mushrooms. Add the fish trimmings, 1 fresh dill sprig, 1.2 litres/2 pints/5 cups water and 120ml/4fl oz/½ cup dry white wine. Bring to the boil, then simmer for 20 minutes, occasionally skimming the surface to remove any fat. Strain through a fine sieve.

FRESH VEGETABLE STOCK (N)

To make about 1 litre/1¾ pints/ 4 cups vegetable stock, chop 225g/8oz carrots, 225g/8oz celery, 1 large onion, 1 leek and ½ fennel bulb into small dice. Melt 25g/1oz/2 tbsp unsalted butter in a large, heavy-based saucepan and fry the vegetables together with 1 fresh bay leaf, 1 fresh thyme sprig, 1 small bunch parsley, 1 crushed garlic clove, 5 black peppercorns and a pinch of sea salt over a gentle heat for about 8 minutes, stirring occasionally. Add 1.2 litres/2 pints/5 cups water and simmer for 30 minutes. Pour the stock through a sieve, squeezing out all the vegetable juices with the back of a wooden spoon.

STARTERS AND SOUPS

*A colourful selection of raw vegetables
and salad leaves is the most satisfying
and healthy way to start each meal.
Choose only the freshest seasonal
varieties, prepared and served
immediately for the best flavour. Serve
with Tahini Tofu Dressing followed by
a protein main course or Soured Cream
and Avocado Dipping Sauce with any
starch dish. Warming Italian Rocket
and Potato Soup is ideal for winter
lunches or as a nutritious supper. And,
if you double the portions for Thai Fish
Soup, it makes a fragrantly flavoured
protein main course.*

Soured Cream and Avocado Dipping Sauce (N)

Serve with Vegetable Salad (see below) as a neutral starter before any main course, or with crisp rounds of toasted pitta bread before a starch main course.

INGREDIENTS

Serves 4
1 large ripe avocado
10 fresh chives
juice of 1 lime
25g/1oz fresh coriander
15ml/1 tbsp finely chopped
    spring onion
45ml/3 tbsp soured cream
salt and freshly ground black pepper
shreds of spring onions, to garnish

1 Place the avocado in a pan of boiling water and turn continuously for one minute. Remove from the pan and peel away the skin – it should come off easily. Cut the avocado in half and remove the stone.

2 Mash the avocado in a bowl with a fork until the flesh is completely smooth, then snip in the fresh chives.

3 Stir in the lime juice, coriander and spring onion and mix well, then fold in the soured cream and seasoning. Chill for 1 hour before serving, garnished with spring onion shreds.

Vegetable Salad (N) with Tahini Tofu Dressing (P)

Choose fresh raw vegetables and salad leaves that are in season and, if possible, buy organic varieties (or better still, grow your own). Serve this neutral salad and protein dressing before any neutral or protein main course.

INGREDIENTS

Serves 4
500g/1¼lb mixed young raw
    vegetables, prepared

For the dressing
1 garlic clove
50ml/2fl oz/¼ cup tahini
115g/4oz soft silken tofu
30ml/2 tbsp lemon juice
50ml/2fl oz/¼ cup sunflower oil
1 spring onion, finely chopped
15ml/1 tbsp light soy sauce
about 50ml/2fl oz/¼ cup water
2.5ml/½ tsp finely ground salt

1 Crush the garlic with the flat side of a knife blade, place in a small bowl and stir in the tahini. Stir in the tofu and lemon juice and then slowly drizzle in the oil.

2 Add the spring onion, reserving a few of the green leaves as a garnish. Add the soy sauce and stir in enough water to make a smooth, thick cream. Season with salt and spoon into a bowl. Garnish with the reserved spring onion and serve with the prepared vegetables.

--- COOK'S TIP ---

This dressing can be made in a blender or food processor if liked. Store in a screw-top jar in the fridge for up to a week.

Fresh Coriander and Yogurt Dipping Sauce (P)

Coriander is the most widely used herb and features in Indian, Mexican, Chinese, Indonesian, Middle Eastern and Caribbean cooking. It is now generally available in supermarkets.

INGREDIENTS

Serves 4

25g/1oz fresh coriander
1 garlic clove
1 small shallot, chopped finely
120ml/4fl oz/½ cup Greek yogurt
salt and freshly ground black pepper
fresh coriander sprig, to garnish
 (optional)

COOK'S TIP

This sauce will keep for 48 hours if stored in a covered container in the fridge.

1 Chop the coriander using a *hachoir* or very sharp knife.

2 Using the flat side of a knife blade, crush the garlic with a little salt to absorb the flavour.

3 Mix the coriander, garlic, shallot and yogurt in a bowl and season to taste with salt and pepper.

4 Spoon into a small serving dish or jar. Serve garnished with a sprig of coriander, if you wish.

Right, clockwise from top left: Fresh Coriander and Yogurt Dipping Sauce, Saffron-flavoured Mayonnaise, Fresh Mayonnaise and Herb-flavoured Mayonnaise.

Fresh Mayonnaise (N)

Fresh mayonnaise is a wonderful, versatile dressing. Since it is a neutral food, it can be used for both starch and protein salads.

INGREDIENTS

Serves 4

2 large egg yolks (preferably
 free-range)
2.5ml/½ tsp salt
5ml/1 tsp Dijon mustard
5ml/1 tsp finely grated lemon rind
 (preferably from an unwaxed lemon)
150ml/¼ pint/⅔ cup sunflower oil

VARIATIONS

Add finely chopped mixed fresh herbs, or 2.5ml/½ tsp saffron threads that have been soaked in 15ml/1 tbsp water.

1 Whisk the egg yolks together with the salt, mustard and lemon rind.

2 Add the oil in a slow drizzle, whisking continuously. Do this very slowly at first, so that each drop of oil is incorporated. As the mayonnaise begins to thicken, add the oil in a slow and steady stream. Adjust the seasoning, then spoon the mayonnaise into a serving dish or jar. Mayonnaise can be kept in the fridge for 3–4 days. Serve at room temperature.

Gazpacho Salsa (N)

Freshly made salsa is delicious with simply grilled or barbecued fish. If you can, use home-grown tomatoes for the best flavour. Failing this, pay a little extra for organic tomatoes or buy one of the super-sweet varieties.

INGREDIENTS

Serves 4
½ large or 1 small cucumber
1 small red onion
450g/1lb firm tomatoes, peeled and seeded
1 large yellow pepper
2 fresh red chillies
1 garlic clove, finely chopped
15ml/1 tbsp finely chopped fresh flat leaf parsley
30ml/2 tbsp finely chopped fresh coriander
30ml/2 tbsp extra virgin olive oil
15ml/1 tbsp cider vinegar
salt and freshly ground black pepper

1 Cut the cucumber in half lengthways. Using a teaspoon, remove and discard the seeds and then cut the flesh into small cubes.

2 Chop the onion and tomatoes into small pieces. Quarter the pepper, discard the seeds and core and cut into small cubes.

3 Finely chop the chillies, discarding the seeds and core.

4 Place all the vegetables in a large bowl and add the garlic, herbs, olive oil, vinegar and seasoning. Mix together thoroughly and then chill in the fridge for 1 hour. Strain off any excess juices and serve.

Anchovy and Parsley Relish (P)

Anchovies and parsley make a flavourful relish to serve as a topping for fresh vegetables.

INGREDIENTS

Serves 4
50g/2oz flat leaf parsley
50g/2oz black olives, stoned
25g/1oz sun-dried tomatoes
4 canned anchovy fillets, drained
50g/2oz red onion, finely chopped
25g/1oz small pickled capers, rinsed
1 garlic clove, finely chopped
15ml/1 tbsp olive oil
juice of ½ lime
1.5ml/¼ tsp ground black pepper
a selection of cherry tomatoes, celery and cucumber, to serve

1 Coarsely chop the parsley, black olives, sun-dried tomatoes and anchovy fillets and mix in a bowl with the onion, capers, garlic, olive oil, lime juice and black pepper.

2 Halve the cherry tomatoes, cut the celery into bite-size chunks and cut the cucumber into 1cm/½ in slices. Top each of the prepared vegetables with a generous amount of relish and serve.

Italian Rocket and Potato Soup (S)

This filling and hearty soup is based on a traditional Italian peasant recipe. If rocket is unavailable, watercress or baby spinach leaves make an equally delicious alternative.

INGREDIENTS

Serves 4

900g/2lb new potatoes
900ml/1½ pints/3¾ cups well-flavoured vegetable stock
1 medium carrot
115g/4oz rocket
2.5ml/½ tsp cayenne pepper
½ loaf stale ciabatta bread, torn into chunks
4 garlic cloves, thinly sliced
60ml/4 tbsp olive oil
salt and freshly ground black pepper

1 Dice the potatoes, then place them in a saucepan with the stock and a little salt. Bring to the boil and simmer for 10 minutes.

— COOK'S TIP —

Garlic burns very easily, so keep your eye on the pan!

2 Finely dice the carrot and add to the potatoes and stock, then tear the rocket leaves and drop into the pan. Simmer for a further 15 minutes, until the vegetables are tender.

3 Add the cayenne pepper and seasoning, then add the chunks of bread. Remove the pan from the heat, then cover and leave to stand for about 10 minutes.

4 Meanwhile sauté the garlic in the olive oil until golden brown. Pour the soup into bowls, add a little of the sautéed garlic to each bowl and serve.

Cream of Grilled Pepper Soup (N)

Weight for weight red and yellow peppers have four times as much Vitamin C as oranges. This is a light, creamy and nutritious soup. Serve with Vegetable Chips instead of Melba toast to serve before a fish main course.

INGREDIENTS

Serves 4

3 large red peppers, halved and seeded
1 large yellow pepper, halved and seeded
15ml/1 tbsp olive oil
1 small shallot, chopped
600ml/1 pint/2½ cups vegetable stock
2 garlic cloves, crushed
1.5ml/¼ tsp saffron strands
150ml/4fl oz/½ cup single cream
475ml/16fl oz/2 cups water
salt and freshly ground black pepper
sprigs of fresh chervil or flat leaf parsley, to garnish
Melba toast, to serve

1 Arrange the peppers skin side up on a baking tray and place under a very hot grill. Grill the peppers until the skin is blackened and blistered and then place them in a plastic bag, knot the end and leave until cool enough to handle. Peel away the skins, reserve one quarter each of a red and yellow pepper and chop the remaining peppers into rough pieces.

2 Heat the oil in a heavy-based saucepan and sauté the shallot until transparent and soft. Add the vegetable stock, garlic, saffron and chopped peppers. Bring to the boil and simmer for 15 minutes.

3 Cool for 10 minutes and then process in a blender or food processor until smooth.

— COOK'S TIP —

If possible, use home-made vegetable stock, or stock made from a good-quality stock cube or bouillon powder.

4 Return the soup to a clean pan. Mix together the cream and water and add to the soup with salt and pepper. Reheat gently without boiling. Pour the soup into bowls and garnish with thin strips of the reserved peppers and sprigs of chervil or flat leaf parsley. Serve with Melba toast.

Thai Fish Soup (P)

Nam pla is a Thai fish sauce, rich in B vitamins, that is used extensively in Thai cooking. It is available at Thai or Indonesian shops and good supermarkets.

INGREDIENTS

Serves 4

350g/12oz raw large prawns
1 lime
15ml/1 tbsp groundnut oil
1.2 litres/2 pints/5 cups well-flavoured
  chicken or fish stock
1 lemon grass stalk, bruised, cut into
  2.5cm/1in lengths
2 kaffir lime leaves, torn into pieces
½ fresh green chilli, seeded and
  finely sliced
4 scallops
24 mussels, scrubbed
115g/4oz monkfish fillet, cut into
  2cm/¾in chunks
10ml/2 tsp *nam pla*
1 kaffir lime leaf, ½ red chilli, ½ lemon
  grass stalk, all finely sliced, to garnish

1 Peel the prawns, reserving the shells, and remove the black thread along the back. Grate the lime rind and squeeze the juice.

2 Heat the oil in a saucepan and fry the prawn shells until pink. Add the chicken or fish stock, lemon grass, kaffir lime leaves, lime rind and sliced green chilli. Bring to the boil, simmer for 20 minutes and then strain through a fine sieve, reserving the liquid.

3 Prepare the scallops by cutting them in half, leaving the corals attached to one half.

4 Return the stock to a clean pan, add the prawns, mussels, monkfish and scallops and cook for 3 minutes. Remove from the heat and add the lime juice and *nam pla*.

5 Serve garnished with finely sliced red chilli, lemon grass and the kaffir lime leaf.

--- COOK'S TIP ---

Double the quantity of fish and seafood to serve as a protein main course.

Star-gazer Vegetable Soup (S)

If you have the time, it is worth making your own stock for this recipe – either vegetable or, if preferred, chicken or fish.

INGREDIENTS

Serves 4

1 yellow pepper
2 large courgettes
2 large carrots
1 kohlrabi
900ml/1½ pints/3¾ cups well-
   flavoured vegetable stock
50g/2oz rice vermicelli
salt and freshly ground black pepper

1 Cut the pepper into quarters, removing the seeds and core. Cut the courgettes and carrots lengthways into 5mm/¼in slices and slice the kohlrabi into 5mm/¼in rounds.

2 Using tiny pastry cutters, stamp out shapes from the vegetables or use a very sharp knife to fashion the sliced vegetables into stars, and other decorative shapes.

COOK'S TIP

Sauté the remaining vegetable pieces in a little oil and mix with cooked brown rice to make a tasty risotto.

3 Place the vegetables and stock in a pan and simmer for 10 minutes. Season to taste with salt and pepper.

4 Meanwhile, place the vermicelli in a bowl, cover with boiling water and set aside for 4 minutes. Drain, divide among four warmed soup bowls and ladle over the soup.

MEAT AND POULTRY

You don't have to be a vegetarian to enjoy a healthy diet, and if you do buy meat choose lean fresh and preferably organic meats or poultry and game with the skin removed. Free-range chicken has a delicate flavour and, when lightly poached in an aromatic broth, makes a delightful summer lunch, served with a sharp mustard mayonnaise. Chicken is delicious with Thai-inspired creamy coconut sauce or stir-fried with Chinese sauces, fresh ginger and lime. For special occasions, entertain your guests with Pheasant Breasts gently flavoured with caramelized apples or crispy duck breasts and pak choi.

Pork Fillet with Red Pepper and Pine Nuts (P)

Pork fillet, also known as tenderloin, is a very lean and inexpensive cut of meat. The tasty stuffing not only adds flavour, but it also keeps the meat moist during cooking. Serve with vegetable purée and lots of lightly steamed broccoli.

INGREDIENTS

Serves 4

60ml/4 tbsp groundnut oil
2 shallots, finely chopped
4 garlic cloves, finely chopped
2 red peppers, seeded and cut into
   small pieces
50g/2oz/½ cup pine nuts
15ml/1 tbsp chopped fresh chervil
2 pork fillets, about 375g/12oz each
300ml/½ pint/1¼ cups medium-dry
   white wine
300ml/½ pint/1¼ cups chicken stock
5ml/1 tsp saffron threads
salt and freshly ground black pepper
sprigs of fresh chervil, to garnish

1 Preheat the oven to 190°C/375°F/Gas 5. Heat 30ml/2 tbsp of the oil in a large heavy-based ovenproof frying pan. Add the shallots and fry gently for 4 minutes until soft, then stir in the garlic, peppers and pine nuts and sauté for a further 5 minutes, stirring occasionally. Remove from the heat and add the chervil and seasoning.

2 Split each pork fillet lengthways without cutting right through and open up each one like a book. Place the pork fillets between two sheets of clear film and lightly flatten with a rolling pin.

3 Spoon the pepper mixture down the centre of each pork fillet. Fold the meat carefully over the filling and secure with cotton string tied at 2.5cm/1in intervals.

4 Heat the remaining oil in the frying pan and fry the fillets for a few minutes until evenly brown. Add the wine, stock and saffron, then cover and bake for about 25 minutes or until the meat is cooked through. Remove the lid or foil and cook, uncovered, for a further 10 minutes to brown.

5 Transfer the pork fillets to a serving plate and keep warm. Pour the cooking liquid into a saucepan, bring to the boil and cook until reduced by half. Season to taste and pour into a serving jug.

6 Slice the meat thickly, remembering to remove the string, and serve with the sauce, garnished with sprigs of fresh chervil.

Pheasant Breasts with Caramelized Apples (P)

Game is a free-range meat that is naturally low in saturated fat and by cooking the pheasant breasts quickly and gently, they retain all their tenderness and flavour. Use free-range chicken breasts when pheasant is unavailable or for a more economical meal.

INGREDIENTS

Serves 4

4 pheasant breasts, about 175g/6oz
   each, skinned
50g/2oz/4 tbsp unsalted butter
5ml/1 tsp icing sugar
3 Granny Smith apples, peeled, cored
   and quartered
10–12 small button mushrooms
300ml/½ pint/1¼ cups dry cider
300ml/½ pint/1¼ cups chicken stock
175ml/6fl oz/¾ cup double cream
5ml/1 tsp freshly squeezed lemon juice
5ml/1 tsp chopped fresh thyme leaves
30ml/2 tbsp chopped fresh parsley
salt and freshly ground black pepper

1 Season the pheasant breasts with salt and pepper. Melt 25g/1oz/ 2 tbsp of the butter in a frying pan and cook the pheasant breasts in batches for about 3 minutes each side. Transfer to a plate with a slotted spoon.

2 Heat the remaining butter and add the icing sugar and apples. Fry gently for 3 minutes until the apples are lightly golden. Transfer to the plate with the pheasant breasts.

3 Add the mushrooms to the pan and stir-fry until all the butter has been absorbed.

4 Add the cider and boil for 3–5 minutes until the liquid has almost completely evaporated. Add the chicken stock and simmer until reduced by half. Stir in the cream and heat gently to boiling point.

5 Return the pheasant breasts and apples to the pan and cook over a low heat for 2 minutes. Stir in the lemon juice, thyme and half of the parsley and season with salt and pepper.

6 Arrange the pheasant breasts on four serving plates and pour the sauce over. Sprinkle with the remaining parsley and serve.

Grilled Spiced Chicken (P)

This dish is delicious served with Fresh Coriander and Yogurt Dipping Sauce and generous portions of very lightly stir-fried green vegetables, such as mangetouts, green beans, broccoli or Chinese cabbage.

INGREDIENTS

Serves 4
5ml/1 tsp coriander seeds
5ml/1 tsp cumin seeds
2 limes
2 garlic cloves, crushed
60ml/4 tbsp chopped fresh coriander
1 small green chilli, seeded and
  finely chopped
30ml/2 tbsp light soy sauce
60ml/4 tbsp sunflower oil
4 boned and skinned chicken breasts,
  about 175g/6oz each
green vegetables, to serve

1 Crush the coriander and cumin seeds using a pestle and mortar or a herb or coffee grinder.

2 Cut the rind from the limes into thin shreds using a zester, avoiding using the pith. Squeeze out the juice from both fruits.

3 Blend the crushed spices, lime rind and juice, garlic, fresh coriander, chilli, soy sauce and oil in a shallow bowl. Add the chicken, turn to coat thoroughly, then cover with clear film and marinate in the fridge for 24 hours.

4 Remove the chicken from the marinade. Heat a grill or griddle pan and cook the chicken for about 4–6 minutes on each side, or until cooked through. Serve with green vegetables.

Moroccan Lamb Kebabs (P)

If you do not have skewers, make small patties instead. The patties can be grilled in exactly the same way as kebabs.

INGREDIENTS

Serves 4
450g/1lb lean lamb, minced
45ml/3 tbsp grated raw onion
15ml/1 tbsp chopped fresh coriander
15ml/1 tbsp chopped fresh parsley
5ml/1 tsp ground cumin
2.5ml/½ tsp chilli powder
1.5ml/¼ tsp ground cinnamon
1.5ml/¼ tsp ground ginger
15ml/1 tbsp raisins
1 egg
salt and freshly ground black pepper
grilled lemon halves and sprigs of fresh
  coriander, to garnish

1 Place the lamb, onion, herbs, spices, raisins, egg and seasoning in a blender or food processor and process for 10–20 seconds or until well blended. Do not over-process. If you do not have a food processor, lightly beat the egg in a bowl, add the other ingredients and mix thoroughly.

2 Form the mixture into cigar shapes about 10cm/4in long and place on a plate. Cover with clear film and chill for about 1 hour.

3 Soak 12 wooden skewers in water for 30 minutes. Push a skewer through each of the lamb "cigars", patting the meat around the skewers to retain the shape.

4 Grill for 5–6 minutes, then turn over the kebabs and cook for a further 5–6 minutes until the meat is evenly browned and cooked through. Serve garnished with grilled lemon halves and sprigs of fresh coriander.

Chicken and Coconut Curry (P)

INGREDIENTS

Serves 4

30ml/2 tbsp groundnut oil
1 large onion, finely chopped
2 bay leaves
2 cinnamon sticks
4 cloves
4 cardamom pods, split
5ml/1 tsp salt
5ml/1 tsp ground cumin
2.5ml/½ tsp ground turmeric
5ml/1 tsp paprika
5ml/1 tsp ground coriander
3 garlic cloves, finely chopped
2.5cm/1in piece fresh root ginger,
    peeled and finely chopped
4 boned and skinned chicken breasts,
    about 225g/8oz each, cut into
    2cm/¾in pieces
45ml/3 tbsp unsweetened coconut
    cream powder
300ml/½ pint/1¼ cups natural yogurt
2.5ml/½ tsp freshly ground black
    pepper
115g/4oz/1 cup frozen petits pois
fresh coriander leaves, to garnish

1 Heat the oil in a large heavy-based saucepan and fry the onion for 5–6 minutes until transparent, stirring frequently. Add the bay leaves, cinnamon sticks, cloves, cardamom pods, salt, cumin, turmeric, paprika and ground coriander and stir well. Cook over a gentle heat for 2–3 minutes, stirring frequently.

2 Stir in the garlic, ginger and chicken pieces and cook over a gentle heat for 3–4 minutes to brown the chicken.

COOK'S TIP

Serve with lightly steamed Chinese leaves or mangetouts.

---

3 Meanwhile, blend the coconut powder with 300ml/½ pint/ 1¼ cups cold water, stirring thoroughly to remove any lumps. Pour into the pan and cook, uncovered, for about 20 minutes, stirring occasionally until the chicken is cooked and the sauce is thick and well reduced.

4 Stir in the yogurt, black pepper and petits pois, and simmer for a further 10 minutes.

5 Spoon the curry into a warmed serving dish or divide among four serving plates, discarding the bay leaves and cinnamon sticks. Garnish with fresh coriander and serve.

Poached Chicken with Mustard Mayonnaise (P)

INGREDIENTS

Serves 4

1 leek, trimmed
1 large carrot
1 celery stick
1 medium onion
1.5kg/3–3½lb free-range chicken,
  washed, without giblets
15ml/1 tbsp roughly chopped
  fresh parsley
10ml/2 tsp roughly chopped
  fresh thyme
6 fresh green peppercorns
mustard mayonnaise, green salad and
  lightly cooked baby carrots, to serve

1 Roughly chop the leek, carrot, celery and onion and place in a large saucepan.

2 Place the chicken on top of the vegetables, cover with water and bring to the boil. Remove any scum that comes to the surface.

3 Add the herbs and peppercorns. Simmer gently for 1 hour. Remove from the heat and cool in the broth.

4 Transfer the chicken to a board or plate and carve, removing the skin. Arrange the slices on a serving platter. Serve with mustard mayonnaise, green salad and lightly cooked baby carrots.

Stir-fried Chicken with Lime and Ginger (P)

Here's a dish that can be prepared in advance and then cooked in minutes. Hoisin sauce is a thick, sweet soya bean sauce available at most supermarkets.

INGREDIENTS

Serves 4

30ml/2 tbsp hoisin sauce
30ml/2 tbsp clear honey
juice of 1 lime
675g/1½lb boned and skinned
  chicken fillet, cut into thin strips
90ml/6 tbsp groundnut oil
1 carrot, cut into thin strips
5cm/2in fresh root ginger, peeled and
  cut into thin strips
30ml/2 tbsp light soy sauce
1 lime, thinly sliced

1 Blend the hoisin sauce, honey and lime juice in a large bowl and add the chicken strips, stirring well. Cover and place in the fridge for 1–2 hours to marinate.

2 Heat the oil in a wok or large frying pan until very hot and almost smoking, and then stir-fry the carrot and ginger until crisp and golden. Transfer with a slotted spoon to a plate lined with kitchen paper.

VARIATION

This is also delicious with stir-fried broccoli, Chinese leaves and toasted almonds.

3 Pour away half the oil from the pan, then add the chicken and stir-fry for about 3–5 minutes until the chicken is cooked through and browned. Add the soy sauce and lime slices, stirring constantly. Serve with the shreds of fried ginger and carrot scattered on top of the chicken.

Crispy Duck Breasts with Pak Choi (P)

If possible, use wild duck for this recipe. It is in season from the beginning of September to the end of January and is much leaner and tastier than the more fatty farmyard ducks. Pak choi (or bok choi), also known as mustard greens, is a type of Chinese cabbage.

INGREDIENTS

Serves 4

4 magrets of duck (breasts), about
  175g/6oz each
450g/1lb pak choi
4 spring onions, trimmed
45ml/3 tbsp light soy sauce
30ml/2 tbsp lemon juice
10ml/2 tsp English mustard, blended
  with 10ml/2 tsp cold water
1cm/½in fresh root ginger, peeled and
  finely shredded
salt and freshly ground black pepper

1 Prick the skin of the duck breasts all over with a fork and rub well with salt and pepper. Heat a heavy-based frying pan, place the breasts in it skin side down and fry undisturbed for 12–14 minutes over a very low heat.

2 Meanwhile remove any tough pak choi stalks and cut the spring onions into diagonal 2.5cm/1in lengths. Blanch the pak choi and onions in lightly salted water for about 1 minute or until the pak choi wilts. Then immerse in very cold water for 30 seconds and drain well. Squeeze out excess water and fluff out the leaves.

3 Mix the soy sauce, lemon juice, mustard and ginger together in a large bowl, add the pak choi and toss to mix. Place the leaves in four bowls.

4 Turn over the duck breasts and fry on the other side for 3 minutes. Preheat the grill and grill the duck, skin side up, for 2–3 minutes until the skin is brown and crisp.

5 Leave the meat to stand for about 5 minutes before carving, then slice each breast crossways in half or into 4–6 pieces. Serve with the pak choi.

FISH AND SEAFOOD

Although most fish and seafood are available all year round, many varieties have a natural season when they are plentiful and have the best flavour. You don't need masses of other ingredients to make fish as wonderfully different as roasted cod with its smooth fresh tomato sauce or grilled salmon served with a super-easy yogurt sauce subtly flavoured with fresh mint and cucumber. Whole sea bass baked "en papillote" is simplicity itself – the paper parcel conserves all its aromatic juices, which are released only as you serve the fish.

Roasted Cod with Fresh Tomato Sauce (P)

Really fresh cod has a sweet, delicate flavour and a pure white flaky flesh. Served with an aromatic tomato sauce, it provides a nutritious meal.

INGREDIENTS

Serves 4

350g/12oz fresh ripe plum tomatoes
75ml/5 tbsp olive oil
2.5ml/½ tsp caster sugar
2 strips of orange rind
1 fresh thyme sprig
6 fresh basil leaves
900g/2lb fresh cod fillet with skin
salt and freshly ground black pepper
steamed green beans, to serve

1 Preheat the oven to 230°C/450°F/ Gas 8. Roughly chop the tomatoes.

2 Heat 15ml/1 tbsp of the olive oil in a heavy-based saucepan, add the tomatoes, sugar, orange rind, thyme and basil and simmer for 5 minutes until the tomatoes are soft.

3 Press the tomato mixture through a fine sieve, discarding the tomato skins and seeds, orange rind and hard pieces of thyme. Pour into a small saucepan and heat gently.

4 Scale the cod fillet and cut on the diagonal into four equal pieces. Season well with salt and pepper.

5 Heat the remaining oil in a clean heavy-based frying pan and fry the cod, skin side down, until the skin is crisp. Place the fish on a greased baking sheet, skin side up, and roast in the oven for 8–10 minutes until the fish is cooked through. Serve the fish on the steamed green beans with the tomato sauce drizzled over it.

Haddock in Spinach Parcels with Pepper Purée (P)

This recipe really deserves a freshly made fish stock, but stock made from vegetable bouillon powder is preferable to most stock cubes. It is delicious served with a sweet pepper purée.

INGREDIENTS

Serves 4

15ml/1 tbsp olive oil
1 small shallot, sliced
2 garlic cloves, sliced
2 yellow peppers, seeded and chopped
1 fresh thyme sprig
600ml/1 pint/2½ cups fish stock
50ml/2fl oz/¼ cup double cream
4 fresh haddock fillets, about 175g/6oz each, skinned
8 large spinach leaves, blanched
salt and freshly ground black pepper

1 Heat the oil in a heavy-based pan and fry the shallot and garlic for 3 minutes, stirring frequently. Add the peppers, thyme and 475ml/16fl oz/2 cups of the fish stock. Season with salt and pepper, then simmer for 15 minutes until the peppers are tender.

2 Place the pepper mixture in a blender or food processor, then process until smooth. Stir in the cream, then pour into a clean saucepan and heat gently to warm through.

3 Meanwhile, half-wrap each fish fillet in two of the blanched spinach leaves. Place the remaining stock in a pan and bring to the boil. Place the fish packages in a steamer, season, then set over the stock and steam for 4 minutes. Arrange the fish parcels on four warmed serving plates and serve with the warm sauce.

COOK'S TIP

To blanch spinach leaves, place them in a colander and pour over boiling water. Plunge them immediately into ice-cold water to set the colour.

Stuffed Sardines with Fresh Rosemary (P)

If fresh sardines are not available, choose four small herrings or two mackerel – they are also delicious cooked this way.

INGREDIENTS

Serves 4
15ml/1 tbsp olive oil
1.5kg/3lb fresh sardines
1 large sprig fresh rosemary
45ml/3 tbsp chopped fresh parsley
1 shallot, finely chopped
115g/4oz/1 cup pine nuts
2 garlic cloves, finely chopped
juice and finely grated rind of
    1 large lemon
salt and freshly ground black pepper
lemon wedges and sprigs of fresh
    rosemary, to garnish

1 Preheat the oven to 190°C/375°F/ Gas 5 and brush an ovenproof dish with a little of the olive oil. Remove the heads of the sardines and split each one down the belly.

2 Place the fish on a chopping board, cut side down, and gently but firmly press down on the backbone. Turn them over and ease out the backbone. Wash the fish well in salted water and pat dry.

3 Pull away the rosemary leaves from the stem and chop finely. Place in a bowl and mix with the parsley, shallot, pine nuts and garlic.

4 Season the fish inside and out with salt and pepper and place a spoonful or two of stuffing inside each one. Press the sides around the stuffing and place each fish in the baking dish.

5 Sprinkle over the remaining olive oil and bake for 30 minutes. Just before serving, squeeze over the lemon juice and sprinkle with the lemon rind. Garnish with lemon wedges and sprigs of rosemary.

Fried Monkfish with Home-made Tapenade (P)

INGREDIENTS

Serves 3–4
450g/1lb fresh monkfish fillet
30ml/2 tbsp olive oil
salt and freshly ground black pepper
chopped fresh parsley and diced red
    pepper, to garnish

For the tapenade
450g/1lb black olives, stoned
75g/3oz capers, drained and rinsed
75g/3oz canned anchovy fillets,
    drained and diced
15ml/1 tbsp Dijon mustard
10 fresh basil leaves, roughly torn
4 garlic cloves, crushed
about 120ml/4fl oz/½ cup extra virgin
    olive oil
15ml/1 tbsp brandy
2.5ml/½ tsp freshly ground
    black pepper

1 To make the tapenade, place all the ingredients in a blender or food processor and process until the mixture is well blended but still has a little texture, adding a little extra olive oil if necessary. You will need about half of the mixture for this recipe – store the remainder in the fridge in a screw-top jar.

2 Cut the fish into rounds about 2.5cm/1in thick. Season with salt and pepper.

3 Heat the olive oil in a heavy-based frying pan and fry the fish on one side for 2 minutes. Turn the fish over and cook for a further 1 minute.

4 Place a generous spoonful of tapenade in the centre of four serving plates and arrange the fish around each mound. Sprinkle with parsley and diced red pepper and serve.

Whole Sea Bass en Papillote (P)

Sea bass is also known as sea wolf, sea dace or sea perch and has delicate pink flesh and a light sweet smell. Cooking in baking paper means the fish retains its flavour. Mullet and bream can be cooked in the same way.

INGREDIENTS

Serves 4
1.5kg/3–3½lb fresh whole sea bass, cleaned, scaled and head removed
5 fresh mint sprigs
½ lemon, sliced
2 shallots, finely sliced
2 fresh plum tomatoes, sliced
45ml/3 tbsp olive oil
salt and freshly ground black pepper
steamed broccoli, to serve

1 Preheat the oven to 175°C/350°F/ Gas 4. Wash and dry the fish and place on a double piece of non-stick baking paper, large enough to wrap the fish comfortably.

2 Season the fish inside and out with salt and pepper.

3 Tuck the fresh mint sprigs, lemon slices, shallots and tomato slices inside the fish and drizzle the olive oil over its back.

4 Fold the paper over the fish and double fold the three open edges.

5 Place the fish on a baking sheet and bake for 40–50 minutes until cooked through. Cut the package open with scissors and serve the fish with steamed broccoli.

Salmon with Yogurt and Mint Dressing (P)

Salmon is a very rich fish and is delicious, grilled and served with this light and delicate sauce. A mixed green leaf and herb salad makes a perfect accompaniment.

INGREDIENTS

Serves 4

½ large cucumber
6 fresh mint leaves
150ml/¼ pint/⅔ cup natural
   Greek yogurt
675g/1½ lb fresh salmon fillet, middle
   cut with skin
5ml/1 tsp olive oil
salt and freshly ground black pepper
mint sprigs, to garnish
fresh spinach leaves, to serve

1 Peel the cucumber, slice in half lengthways and remove the seeds.

2 Grate the cucumber into a sieve, salt lightly and drain for about 30 minutes. Chop the mint leaves.

3 Place the chopped mint leaves in a bowl with the yogurt. Squeeze out any excess juice from the cucumber and stir into the bowl with the yogurt and mint. Season with black pepper.

4 Preheat the grill until moderately hot. Scale the salmon if the fishmonger has not already done this and check for any bones. Cut the salmon into four pieces, brush with the olive oil and season with a little salt.

5 Grill the fish for 3 minutes, skin side up, then carefully turn over the fish and grill for about 2 minutes on the other side. The skin should be browned and crisp. Serve on a bed of spinach with the yogurt and cucumber dressing. Garnish with sprigs of mint and grind over some black pepper.

Butterflied Mediterranean Prawns (P)

Skewered prawns, marinated in a fiery herb dressing, then grilled until pink and tender, make a delicious light lunch or summer supper dish.

Ingredients

Serves 4

32 raw king prawns, peeled
2 garlic cloves, finely chopped
90ml/6 tbsp finely chopped
   fresh parsley
1 fresh rosemary sprig, leaves removed
   and finely chopped
pinch of dried chilli flakes
juice of 2 fresh limes
30ml/2 tbsp olive oil
salt and freshly ground black pepper
green salad, to serve

1 Wash the prawns in salted water, remove their heads and shells, then remove the black thread that runs along the back of the prawn. To butterfly the prawns, cut along the back, without completely cutting through, then carefully fan out.

2 Blend the garlic, parsley, rosemary, chilli flakes, lime juice and olive oil in a large bowl. Add the prawns, stir well and leave to marinate for 1 hour.

3 Meanwhile, soak 32 wooden skewers in warm water for at least 30 minutes.

4 Preheat the grill until very hot. Thread 2 prawns on to each pair of skewers and grill for 2–3 minutes until each side has turned bright pink. Remove the prawns from the skewers and serve with green salad.

Seared Scallops with Lemon and Thyme (P)

Scallop shells make attractive little dishes and most good fishmongers will sell you the scallops and shells together. Make sure the shells are well scrubbed and clean before using.

Ingredients

Serves 4

50ml/2fl oz/¼ cup olive oil
2 garlic cloves, finely chopped
4 fresh thyme sprigs
1 bay leaf
15ml/1 tbsp chopped fresh parsley
16 fresh scallops, rinsed
1 shallot, finely chopped
15ml/1 tbsp balsamic vinegar
30ml/2 tbsp lemon juice
150ml/¼ pint/⅔ cup chicken or
   vegetable stock
salt and freshly ground black pepper
24 baby spinach leaves, to garnish

1 Blend the olive oil, garlic, thyme, bay leaf and parsley in a shallow bowl. Add the scallops and leave to marinate in a cool place for 1 hour.

2 Heat a heavy-based frying pan until smoking. Remove the scallops from the marinade and sear for about 30 seconds on each side to seal in their juices. Transfer the scallops to a plate and keep warm.

3 Add the marinade to the pan, then add the shallot and balsamic vinegar, lemon juice and stock. Cook over a high heat for 5 minutes until the stock is well reduced. Discard the bay leaf and season with salt and pepper.

4 Arrange 6 spinach leaves around each scallop shell in the centre of four serving plates, place 4 scallops in each shell and pour over the juices.

Mussels in Fennel and White Wine (P)

INGREDIENTS

Serves 4

1.5kg/3–3½lb fresh mussels
3 shallots
3 garlic cloves
1 small fennel bulb
15ml/1 tbsp olive oil
300ml/½ pint/1¼ cups dry white wine
15ml/1 tbsp chopped fresh parsley
juice of ½ lemon
chopped fresh parsley, to garnish
salt and freshly ground black pepper

— COOK'S TIP —

After you have washed the mussels, give
any that are open a sharp tap, and if they
refuse to close, discard them. Conversely,
any mussels that remain closed after
cooking should also be thrown away.

---

1 Scrub the mussels thoroughly in
several changes of water (see
Cook's Tip) and pull away the beards.
Set the mussels aside.

2 Finely chop the shallots and garlic.
Remove the root from the fennel
and slice finely.

3 Heat the oil in a heavy-based pan
and fry the shallots, fennel and garlic
for 1 minute, stirring all the time. Add
the wine and simmer for 5 minutes.

4 Add the mussels and parsley, cover
with a tight-fitting lid and cook for
4 minutes, shaking the pan occasionally.
Remove the lid and check that all the
mussels are open.

5 Squeeze in the lemon juice, then
season to taste. Divide the mussels
among four large bowls. Pour the
liquid over the mussels and sprinkle
with chopped parsley.

Seafarer's Stew (P)

Any variety of firm fish may be used in this recipe, but be sure to use smoked haddock as well; it is essential for its distinctive flavour.

INGREDIENTS

Serves 4

225g/8oz naturally smoked haddock
    fillet (uncoloured)
225g/8oz fresh monkfish fillet
20 fresh mussels, scrubbed
2 streaky bacon rashers (optional)
15ml/1 tbsp olive oil
1 shallot, finely chopped
225g/8oz carrots, coarsely grated
150ml/¼ pint/⅔ cup single or
    double cream
115g/4oz cooked peeled prawns
salt and freshly ground black pepper
30ml/2 tbsp chopped fresh parsley,
    to garnish

1 In a large heavy-based pan, simmer the haddock and monkfish in 1.2 litres/2 pints/5 cups water for 5 minutes, then add the mussels and cover the pan with a lid.

2 Cook for a further 5 minutes or until all the mussels have opened. Discard any that have not. Drain, reserving the liquid. Return the liquid to the rinsed pan and set aside.

3 Flake the haddock coarsely, removing any skin and bones, then cut the monkfish into large chunks. Cut the bacon, if using, into strips.

4 Heat the oil in a heavy-based frying pan and fry the shallot and bacon for 3–4 minutes or until the shallot is soft and the bacon lightly browned. Add to the strained fish broth, bring to the boil, then add the grated carrots and cook for 10 minutes.

5 Stir in the cream together with the haddock, monkfish, mussels and prawns and heat gently, without boiling. Season and serve in large bowls, garnished with parsley.

COOK'S TIP

The advantage of using double cream is that the liquid will not curdle if you do accidentally let it boil.

VEGETABLES AND SALADS

Vegetables and salads are vital to
healthy eating and should be considered
as an important part of each meal and
not just an occasional accompaniment.
For the finest flavour, choose organic
and seasonal varieties whenever possible.
Stoved Mixed Mushrooms are a meal
in themselves served in a hollowed out
wholemeal bread roll and accompanied
by lots of fresh salad. Celeriac, Turnip
and Carrot Purée is delicious to mop up
the juices of fish or game, and makes a
nutritious meal on its own served with
nutty brown rice generously scattered
with toasted hazelnuts.

Winter Vegetable Ragout (S)

INGREDIENTS

Serves 4
30ml/2 tbsp extra virgin olive oil
1 onion, finely chopped
25g/1oz dried porcini mushrooms,
   rinsed well, then soaked in 300ml/
   ½ pint/1¼ cups hot water
   for 10 minutes
2 garlic cloves, finely chopped
1 fresh thyme sprig
2 bay leaves
4 carrots, cut into 5cm/2in sticks
1 celery stick, sliced
1 small cauliflower, broken
   into florets
2 parsnips, cut into 5cm/2in sticks
2 large potatoes, cubed
115g/4oz button mushrooms
115g/4oz baby Brussels sprouts
salt and freshly ground black pepper
30ml/2 tbsp each chopped fresh parsley
   and tarragon, to garnish

1 Heat the olive oil in a large heavy-based frying pan and fry the onion for 4–5 minutes until golden brown. Drain the mushrooms, reserving the soaking liquid.

2 Add the garlic, thyme, bay leaves, carrots, celery, cauliflower, parsnips and potatoes. Stir well and cook for 2 minutes.

3 Strain the mushroom liquid and add to the pan together with the porcini mushrooms. Cover and cook gently for 10 minutes.

4 Add the button mushrooms and Brussels sprouts and cook for a further 5 minutes until all of the vegetables are tender. Taste and adjust the seasoning, then serve, with the chopped parsley and tarragon sprinkled over the top.

COOK'S TIP

Turn the ragout into a pie by covering it with a thick layer of mashed potatoes. Bake in the oven at 180°C/350°F/Gas 4 for a further 30 minutes until the potatoes are golden brown.

Almost-dry Roasted Vegetables (N)

This is a delicious if rather slow method of cooking vegetables, but they retain all their juicy flavour. Serve them with pasta, hot toast or Grilled Polenta as a starch main course.

INGREDIENTS

Serves 4

1 aubergine
2 courgettes
1 yellow pepper
1 red pepper
4 garlic cloves
1 sweet red onion
1 small fennel bulb
20 small asparagus spears
10 fresh basil leaves, roughly torn
45ml/3 tbsp extra virgin olive oil
15ml/1 tbsp balsamic vinegar
salt and freshly ground black pepper
sprigs of basil, to garnish

1 Preheat the oven to 240°C/475°F/ Gas 9. Cut the aubergine and courgettes into 1cm/½in slices. Halve the peppers, discard the seeds and core, then cut them into chunks.

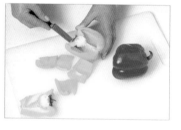

2 Finely chop the garlic and cut the onion into eight wedges.

3 Remove the root from the fennel and slice into 2.5cm/1in strips.

4 Place all the vegetables in a bowl, add the basil, then stir in the olive oil. Season with salt and pepper and mix together well.

5 Tip the vegetables into a shallow roasting dish and roast in the oven for 30–40 minutes until the vegetables are brown on the edges. Leave to cool, then sprinkle with the balsamic vinegar and serve garnished with sprigs of basil.

Celeriac, Turnip and Carrot Purée (N)

This sophisticated, subtly coloured combination of root vegetables is delicious with both meat and fish. Parsnips and swede have stronger flavours and are excellent with pheasant and pork.

INGREDIENTS

Serves 4
225g/8oz celeriac
225g/8oz turnips
225g/8oz carrots
1 small shallot
25g/1oz/2 tbsp butter
15ml/1 tbsp single cream
1.5ml/¼ tsp freshly grated nutmeg
salt and freshly ground black pepper
fresh chives, to garnish

1 Peel the celeriac and peel or scrape the turnips if necessary.

2 Cut the celeriac, turnips and carrots into bite-size pieces and finely chop the shallot. Place in a pan of very lightly salted boiling water. Cook for 8 minutes until tender but still firm.

3 Drain in a colander and place in a blender or food processor with the butter and cream. Process to a fine purée, then season with salt, pepper and nutmeg. Spoon directly into four serving bowls. Garnish with fresh chives and serve immediately.

Stir-fried Green Beans with Ginger (N)

Green beans keep their crunchy texture even after cooking and may be served cold as an alternative salad or as a tasty light starter.

INGREDIENTS

Serves 4
1cm/½in piece fresh root ginger
450g/1lb fresh green beans
30ml/2 tbsp olive oil
2.5ml/½ tsp black mustard seeds
50ml/2fl oz/¼ cup water
2.5ml/½ tsp ground cumin
1.5ml/¼ tsp ground turmeric
30ml/2 tbsp chopped fresh coriander
5ml/1 tsp salt
5ml/1 tsp lemon juice
freshly ground black pepper
shreds of fried ginger, to garnish

1 Peel the ginger and cut into very fine strips. Top and tail the beans and cut in half.

2 Heat the olive oil in a large frying pan, wok or flameproof casserole and sauté the mustard seeds and ginger until the seeds crackle.

3 Add the beans and stir-fry over a medium heat for 5 minutes.

4 Add the water, cover the pan and simmer for 3 minutes. Remove the lid and simmer until almost all the water has evaporated, then add the cumin, turmeric, coriander and salt.

5 Continue cooking until the beans are tender but crisp, and the water has completely evaporated. Add the lemon juice, season with black pepper and garnish with shreds of ginger. Serve at once.

> ——— COOK'S TIP ———
>
> Be careful not to allow the beans to overcook or they will lose their delicious crunchy texture.

Stoved Mixed Mushrooms (S)

Nothing can match the flavour of freshly picked wild mushrooms: the next best thing is to combine several different cultivated types. If possible, choose organically grown mushrooms, which have a richer flavour.

INGREDIENTS

Serves 4
2 garlic cloves
1 shallot
450g/1lb mushrooms, such as oyster, brown-cap, large field, button and ceps
75ml/5 tbsp olive oil
30ml/2 tbsp chopped fresh chervil
30ml/2 tbsp chopped fresh parsley
chopped leaves of 1 fresh rosemary sprig
salt and freshly ground black pepper
sprigs of fresh chervil, to garnish
4 bread rolls, to serve

1 Finely chop the garlic and shallot. Wipe the mushrooms, carefully removing any dirt and discarding any very tough stems. Slice the larger mushrooms and halve the smaller ones.

2 Heat the olive oil in a heavy-based, deep frying pan and fry the shallot over a medium to high heat for about 1 minute.

3 Add the garlic, mushrooms and fresh herbs to the pan and sauté for about 5 minutes. Season to taste. Split open the bread rolls by cutting a cross in the top, then divide the mushrooms among them. Garnish with sprigs of chervil and serve.

VARIATION

For an alternative substantial starch meal, serve the mushrooms with Grilled Polenta or freshly cooked pasta. Served without the bread rolls, this dish is neutral and would make a tasty starter before either a starch or protein main course.

Aubergine and Spinach Terrines (P)

These individual terrines make an elegant first course or accompaniment to either a fish or meat course, cold or hot.

INGREDIENTS

Serves 4

1 aubergine
30ml/2 tbsp extra virgin olive oil
2 courgettes, thinly sliced
leaves from 1 small fresh thyme sprig
4 firm tomatoes, peeled and seeded
4 fresh basil leaves, finely sliced
275g/10oz baby spinach leaves
1 garlic clove, crushed
15g/½oz/1 tbsp butter
pinch of freshly grated nutmeg
salt and freshly ground black pepper
½ roasted red pepper, skinned and
   chopped, plus a little balsamic
   vinegar, to serve

1 Preheat the oven to 190°C/375°F/ Gas 5 and seal four 6cm/2½in diameter metal muffin rings at one end with clear film.

2 Slice the aubergine into four equal-sized rounds. Heat half the oil in a frying pan and fry the aubergines on both sides until brown. Place the aubergines on a baking sheet and cook in the oven for 10 minutes. Transfer to a plate lined with kitchen paper.

3 Heat half the remaining oil in the same pan and fry the courgettes for 2 minutes, then drain on the kitchen paper. Season with salt and pepper and sprinkle with thyme leaves.

4 Place the tomatoes, basil and the rest of the oil in a heavy-based frying pan and cook for 5–8 minutes. Cook the spinach, garlic and butter in a saucepan, allowing all the water to evaporate. Drain and add the nutmeg and season with salt and pepper.

5 Line the base and about 1cm/½ in of the sides of the muffin rings with the spinach leaves, making sure the leaves overlap, leaving no gaps. Place the courgettes around the edges of each ring, overlapping slightly.

6 Divide the tomato mixture equally among the rings, pressing down well. Place the aubergines on the top, trimming the edges to fit.

7 Seal the top with clear film and pierce the base to allow any liquid to escape. Chill overnight. Remove carefully from the rings and serve with diced roasted peppers, drizzled with balsamic vinegar.

COOK'S TIP

Double or triple the quantities in this recipe to make a vegetarian main course and serve with a crisp green salad and a sharp lemon and oil dressing.

Mixed Green Leaf and Herb Salad (N)

Serve this salad as an accompaniment, or turn it into a main course salad by adding one of the variations, right.

INGREDIENTS

Serves 4

15g/¹/₂oz/¹/₂ cup mixed fresh herbs, such as chervil, tarragon (use sparingly), dill, basil, marjoram (use sparingly), flat leaf parsley, mint, sorrel, fennel and coriander
350g/12oz mixed salad leaves, such as rocket, radicchio, chicory, watercress, curly endive, baby spinach, oakleaf lettuce, nasturtium (and the flowers) and dandelion

For the dressing

50ml/2fl oz/¹/₄ cup extra virgin olive oil
15ml/1 tbsp sherry vinegar
salt and freshly ground black pepper

1 Wash and dry the herbs and salad leaves using a salad spinner or place them between two clean, dry dish towels and carefully pat dry.

2 Blend together the oil and vinegar and season well.

3 Place the salad and herbs in a large bowl, add the dressing and mix well using your hands to toss the leaves. The dressing should be added just before serving.

VARIATIONS

For a protein main course, add one of the following:
• Freshly grilled salmon or tuna or cooked peeled prawns, either cold or grilled, and lightly dusted with chilli powder.
• Fat slices of mozzarella cheese with stoned black olives and a few green capers.
• Slivers of Pecorino cheese with bite-size pieces of crisp pear.

For a starch main course, add one of the following:
• Tiny new potatoes in their jackets, crumbled hard-boiled egg yolks, sprouted beansprouts.
• Baby broad beans, sliced artichoke hearts and garlic croûtons.
• Cooked chick-peas, asparagus tips and stoned green olives stuffed with peppers.

Feta and Apple Salad (P)

INGREDIENTS

Serves 4

45ml/3 tbsp olive oil
juice of 1 lime
1.5ml/¹/₂ tsp English mustard
1 red apple
1 green apple
50g/2oz rocket
400g/14oz freshly sprouted seeds and pulses
2 spring onions, finely chopped
5ml/1 tsp chopped fresh basil
10ml/2 tsp snipped fresh chives
10ml/2 tsp chopped fresh chervil
5ml/1 tsp chopped fresh tarragon
30ml/2 tbsp chopped walnuts
175g/6oz feta cheese
salt and freshly ground black pepper

1 Pour the olive oil and lime juice into a large bowl and mix with the mustard, salt and black pepper.

VARIATION

As an alternative to feta, which is rather salty, you could use a milder but still crumbly cheese like Caerphilly.

2 Core the apples, slice into thin shavings and mix with the dressing in the bowl. Add the rocket, sprouted seeds and pulses, spring onions, herbs and walnuts and mix well.

3 Serve in one large serving bowl or in four individual bowls with the feta cheese crumbled on top.

Oriental Salad (N)

This fragrantly flavoured salad combines with either starch or protein meals. The dressing may be used for any combinations of raw vegetables and green salads.

INGREDIENTS

Serves 4

225g/8oz fresh beansprouts
1 cucumber
2 carrots
1 small daikon radish
1 small red onion, thinly sliced
2.5cm/1in fresh root ginger, peeled and
   cut into thin matchsticks
1 small red chilli, seeded and
   thinly sliced
handful of fresh coriander leaves or
   fresh mint leaves

For the oriental dressing

15ml/1 tbsp rice vinegar
15ml/1 tbsp light soy sauce
15ml/1 tbsp *nam pla* (Thai fish sauce)
1 garlic clove, finely chopped
15ml/1 tbsp sesame oil
45ml/3 tbsp groundnut oil
30ml/2 tbsp sesame seeds,
   lightly toasted

1 First make the dressing. Place all the dressing ingredients in a bottle or screw-top jar and shake well.

2 Wash the beansprouts and drain thoroughly in a colander.

3 Peel the cucumber, cut in half lengthways and scoop out the seeds. Peel the cucumber flesh into long ribbon strips using a potato peeler or mandolin.

4 Peel the carrots and radish into long strips in the same way as for the cucumber.

5 Place the carrots, radish and cucumber in a large shallow serving dish, add the onion, ginger, chilli and coriander or mint and toss to mix. Pour the dressing over just before serving.

— COOK'S TIP —

The dressing may be made in advance and will keep well for a couple of days if stored in the fridge or a cool place.

Fennel and Herb Coleslaw (N)

This neutral salad may be adapted into a protein meal with the addition of generous chunks of feta or any other crumbly and salty cheese together with slices of crisp red apples.

INGREDIENTS

Serves 4

175g/6oz fennel
2 spring onions
175g/6oz white cabbage
115g/4oz celery
175g/6oz carrots
50g/2oz sultanas
2.5ml/½ tsp caraway seeds (optional)
15ml/1 tbsp chopped fresh parsley
45ml/3 tbsp extra virgin olive oil
5ml/1 tsp lemon juice
shreds of spring onion, to garnish

1 Using a sharp knife, cut the fennel and spring onions into thin slices.

VARIATION
Use soured cream instead of olive oil for a creamier dressing.

2 Slice the cabbage and celery finely and cut the carrots into fine strips. Place in a serving bowl together with the other vegetables. Add the sultanas and caraway seeds, if using, and toss lightly to mix.

3 Stir in the chopped parsley, olive oil and lemon juice and mix all the ingredients very thoroughly. Cover and chill for 3 hours to allow the flavours to mingle, and then serve, garnished with spring onion shreds.

GRAINS, PULSES AND RICE

*If you have always thought of grains
and pulses as rather dull and stodgy you
will be pleasantly surprised by the
flavour and texture of Cracked Wheat
Salad and Bean Feast with its sharp
and pungent Tomato and Avocado
Salsa. Freshly made Hummus is much
more wholesome and crunchy when
made with sprouted chick-peas and is
irresistible with lots of piping hot
Vegetable Chips. While all these recipes
are indicated as starch dishes, beans and
pulses do contain some protein which is
important for vegetarians.*

Falafels with Tahini Dressing (S)

Falafels or chick-pea rissoles are a popular Middle Eastern snack. Serve them with a green leaf salad and pitta bread.

INGREDIENTS

Serves 4

225g/8oz/1½ cups dried chick-peas, soaked overnight
1 large onion, finely chopped
4 spring onions, finely chopped
45ml/3 tbsp chopped fresh coriander
45ml/3 tbsp chopped fresh parsley
5ml/1 tsp ground coriander
5ml/1 tsp ground fennel seeds
5ml/1 tsp ground cumin
2.5ml/½ tsp baking powder
2 garlic cloves, crushed
sunflower oil, for frying
salt and freshly ground black pepper
pinch of paprika and chopped fresh coriander, to garnish

For the dressing

45ml/3 tbsp tahini

1 Drain the chick-peas and cook in plenty of boiling water for 1–1½ hours until tender.

2 Drain the chick-peas and process in a blender or food processor until they form a smooth paste. Add the onion and spring onions, coriander and parsley, process again for a few seconds and then add the ground spices, baking powder and crushed garlic. Season with salt and pepper.

3 Tip the mixture into a bowl and knead with your hands until pliable, then leave it to rest in the fridge for at least 30 minutes.

4 Meanwhile, make the dressing. Place the tahini in a bowl and gradually add 120ml/4fl oz/½ cup water, to make a smooth paste, the consistency of cream. Season with salt and pepper and spoon into a serving bowl. Chill until ready to serve.

5 Take walnut-size pieces of the mixture and form into small balls about 4cm/1½in across. Heat a little oil in a frying pan and fry the falafels, three or four at a time, for about 3 minutes each side, until lightly browned. Drain on kitchen paper and keep warm. Repeat with the remaining falafels. Arrange on a serving plate, dust with paprika and garnish with fresh coriander. Serve with the tahini dressing.

Hummus with Baked Vegetable Chips (S)

This classic Middle Eastern starter is ideally made using sprouted chick-peas, which are available at health food stores and most good supermarkets. Canned chick-peas are a useful standby and can be used in place of the sprouted chick-peas — rinse them thoroughly before using.

INGREDIENTS

Serves 4
450g/1lb sprouted chick-peas (or 400g/14oz can chick-peas)
2 garlic cloves, crushed
50ml/4 tbsp tahini
60ml/4 tbsp extra virgin olive oil
30ml/2 tbsp lemon juice
salt
small pinch of paprika and sprigs of flat leaf parsley or chervil, to garnish

For the vegetable chips
2 large aubergines
4 large parsnips
5ml/1 tsp extra virgin olive oil

1 Blend the chick-peas in a food processor until completely smooth. Add the garlic, tahini and a little salt.

--- COOK'S TIP ---

To make a rich sauce for steamed vegetables, just add a little more water.

2 With the machine running, slowly pour on the olive oil to make a thick, smooth sauce and then add the lemon juice. If the mixture is too thick, add a little water. Transfer to a serving bowl and set aside in a cool place.

3 Preheat the oven to 120°C/250°F/ Gas ½. Slice the aubergines and parsnips into very thin rounds. Brush both sides of the vegetable slices with olive oil and sprinkle with a little salt.

4 Place on oven racks and bake in the oven for 30 minutes until golden brown and crisp. The vegetables may take longer, so continue cooking, checking every 10 minutes.

5 Serve the vegetable chips with the hummus, garnished with a light dusting of paprika and sprigs of fresh parsley or chervil.

Cracked Wheat Salad with Walnuts and Herbs (S)

INGREDIENTS

Serves 4

225g/8oz/1 generous cup cracked
   wheat
350ml/12fl oz/1½ cups vegetable stock
1 cinnamon stick
generous pinch of ground cumin
pinch of cayenne pepper
pinch of ground cloves
5ml/1 tsp salt, finely ground
10 mangetouts, topped and tailed
1 red and 1 yellow pepper, roasted,
   skinned, seeded and diced
2 plum tomatoes, peeled, seeded
   and diced
2 shallots, finely sliced
5 black olives, stoned and cut
   into quarters
30ml/2 tbsp each shredded fresh basil,
   mint and parsley
30ml/2 tbsp roughly chopped walnuts
30ml/2 tbsp balsamic vinegar
120ml/4fl oz/½ cup extra virgin
   olive oil
freshly ground black pepper
onion rings, to garnish

1 Place the cracked wheat in a large
bowl. Pour the stock into a
saucepan and bring to the boil with the
spices and salt.

COOK'S TIP

To roast the peppers, cut in half and place
skin side up on a baking tray. Place in an
oven preheated to 220°C/425°F/Gas 7 and
roast for about 20 minutes until the skins
are charred. Place the peppers in a plastic
bag, knot the end and leave for 10 minutes.
The skin will then be simply pulled away.

2 Cook for 1 minute, then pour the
stock over the cracked wheat and
leave to stand for 30 minutes.

3 In another bowl, mix together the
mangetouts, peppers, tomatoes,
shallots, olives, herbs and walnuts. Add
the vinegar, olive oil and a little black
pepper and stir thoroughly to mix.

4 Strain the cracked wheat of any
liquid and discard the cinnamon
stick. Place in a serving bowl, stir in the
fresh vegetable mixture and serve,
garnished with onion rings.

Savoy Cabbage and Vegetable Pie (S)

Before cooking the lentils, spread them out on a plate to check there are no pieces of grit, which often occur and can seriously damage your teeth! Serve this pie with baked potatoes, or new potatoes steamed in their jackets.

INGREDIENTS

Serves 4

1 small Savoy cabbage, outer leaves removed
45ml/3 tbsp olive oil
1 shallot, finely chopped
1 garlic clove, finely chopped
1 carrot, cut into small dice
1 leek, white part only, cut into thin slices
1 celery stick, cut into small dice
15ml/1 tbsp pine nuts
1 bay leaf
115g/4oz/½ cup Puy lentils
600ml/1 pint/2½ cups vegetable stock
75ml/5 tbsp double cream
3 egg yolks
salt and freshly ground black pepper

1 Pull away ten large undamaged cabbage leaves and blanch them in saucepan of boiling water for minute. Plunge into a bowl of ice-cold water for 30 seconds and drain immediately.

2 Cut the remaining cabbage into quarters, cut out and discard the talk and slice very thinly.

3 Heat the oil in a heavy-based saucepan and fry the shallot for 3 minutes until softened. Add the garlic, sliced cabbage, carrot, leek, celery, pine nuts and bay leaf and cook for a further 3 minutes, stirring frequently.

4 Add the lentils and vegetable stock to the pan, cover and simmer for about 30 minutes until the lentils are tender and the liquid has evaporated. Leave to cool. Preheat the oven to 200°C/400°F/Gas 6.

5 Line a 15cm/6in flan tin with seven of the cabbage leaves and season with salt and pepper.

6 Blend the cream with the egg yolks and stir into the lentil mixture. Season to taste, then spoon the mixture into the cabbage ring and cover with the remaining leaves. Cover with foil and cook in the oven for 40 minutes. Once the pie is cooked, leave it to stand, still covered with foil, for 10 minutes before slicing into thick wedges to serve.

Wild Rice and Grain Pilaf with Mushrooms (S)

INGREDIENTS

Serves 4

50g/2oz/¼ cup wheat berries
25g/1oz/2 tbsp butter
1 shallot, finely chopped
50g/2oz/¼ cup wild rice
600ml/1 pint/2½ cups vegetable stock
1 bay leaf
50g/2oz/¼ cup brown basmati rice
115g/4oz/1½ cups shiitake mushrooms
115g/4oz/1½ cups brown-cap
  mushrooms
30ml/2 tbsp olive oil
4 spring onions, thinly sliced
50g/2oz/¼ cup hazelnuts, roughly
  chopped
salt and freshly ground black pepper

1 Rinse the wheat berries, cover with 1 litre/1¾ pints/4 cups boiling water and leave to soak for at least 2 hours or overnight. Drain.

2 Melt the butter in a heavy-based frying pan and fry the shallot for 3 minutes. Add the wheat berries and wild rice, stir well to coat the grains, and then add the stock, bay leaf and 2.5ml/½ tsp salt. Bring to the boil, then lower the heat, cover and simmer for 30 minutes.

3 Stir in the brown basmati rice and simmer for a further 20 minutes. Remove from the heat and leave to stand for 5 minutes.

4 Quarter the shiitake mushrooms and remove and discard the stem. Quarter the brown-cap mushrooms. Heat the olive oil in another frying pan and fry the mushrooms for 3 minutes, stirring well. Add the spring onions and hazelnuts and cook for a further 1 minute.

5 Strain any liquid from the rice and then stir in the mushrooms. Season with salt and pepper to taste and serve.

Grilled Polenta (S)

Polenta is coarse yellow maize grain and is one of the staples of northern Italy where it often replaces bread. A couple of slices of grilled polenta with Star-gazer Vegetable Soup and a hearty salad make a well-balanced and satisfying lunch. It is also delicious with Stoved Mixed Mushrooms.

INGREDIENTS
Serves 4
900ml/1½ pints/3¾ cups water
175g/6oz/1¼ cups polenta
25g/1oz/2 tbsp butter
5ml/1 tsp extra virgin olive oil
salt and freshly ground black pepper

1 Boil the water in a large heavy-based saucepan and add 5ml/1 tsp salt. Reduce the heat until the water is just simmering and slowly pour in the polenta, stirring vigorously until completely blended.

2 Reduce the heat further and cook for 40 minutes, stirring every 5 minutes with a wooden spoon. The polenta is cooked when it is very thick and falls away from the sides of the pan.

3 Stir in the butter and seasoning and transfer to a flat baking sheet. Spread out until about 2.5cm/1in thick and set aside until completely cold.

4 Cut the polenta into wedges or slices and brush each piece lightly with olive oil. Place under a hot grill until each slice is crisp and brown on both sides. Serve hot.

Lentil Risotto with Vegetables (S)

INGREDIENTS

Serves 4

45ml/3 tbsp sunflower oil
1 large onion, thinly sliced
2 garlic cloves, crushed
1 large carrot, cut into matchsticks
225g/8oz/1 generous cup brown
   basmati rice, washed and drained
115g/4oz/½ cup green or brown
   lentils, soaked overnight and drained
5ml/1 tsp ground cumin
5ml/1 tsp ground cinnamon
20 black cardamom seeds
6 cloves
600ml/1 pint/2½ cups vegetable stock
2 bay leaves
2 celery sticks
1 large avocado
3 plum tomatoes
salt and freshly ground black pepper
green salad, to serve

1 Heat the oil in a heavy-based pan and fry the onion, garlic and carrot for 5–6 minutes, until the onion is transparent and the carrot is slightly softened.

2 Add the drained rice and lentils together with the cumin, cinnamon, cardamom seeds and cloves and continue frying over a low heat for a further 5 minutes, stirring well to prevent sticking.

3 Add the stock and bay leaves and bring to the boil, then cover the pan and simmer very gently for a further 15 minutes or until the liquid has been absorbed and the rice and lentils are tender. Taste and adjust the seasoning.

4 Meanwhile, chop the celery into half-rounds and dice the avocado and tomatoes.

5 Add the fresh ingredients to the rice and lentils and stir to mix. Spoon into a large serving bowl and serve immediately with a green salad.

Bean Feast with Tomato and Avocado Salsa (S)

This is a super-quick recipe using canned beans, although it could be made with dried beans, which would need to be soaked overnight and then cooked for 1–1½ hours until tender.

INGREDIENTS

Serves 4

400g/14oz can red kidney beans
400g/14oz can flageolet beans
400g/14oz can borlotti beans
15ml/1 tbsp olive oil
1 small onion, finely chopped
3 garlic cloves, finely chopped
1 red Ancho chilli, seeded and
    finely chopped
1 red pepper, seeded and
    coarsely chopped
2 bay leaves
10ml/2 tsp chopped fresh oregano
10ml/2 tsp ground cumin
5ml/1 tsp ground coriander
2.5ml/½ tsp ground cloves
15ml/1 tbsp dark brown sugar
300ml/½ pint/1¼ cups vegetable stock
salt and freshly ground black pepper
sprigs of fresh coriander, to garnish

For the salsa
1 ripe but firm avocado
45ml/3 tbsp fresh lime juice
1 small red onion
1 small hot green chilli
3 ripe plum tomatoes
45ml/3 tbsp chopped fresh coriander

1 Drain the beans in a colander and rinse thoroughly. Heat the oil in a heavy-based saucepan and fry the onion for 3 minutes, until soft and transparent. Add the garlic, chilli, red pepper, herbs and spices.

2 Stir well and cook for a further 3 minutes, then add the sugar, beans and stock and cook for 8 minutes. Season with salt and pepper.

3 To make the salsa, peel the avocado, cut it in half around the stone, then remove the stone using a large sharp knife. Cut the flesh into 1cm/½in dice. Place in a mixing bowl with the lime juice and stir to mix.

4 Roughly chop the onion and finely slice the chilli, discarding the seeds. Plunge the tomatoes into boiling water, leave for 1 minute and then peel away the skin. Chop the tomatoes into rough pieces and discard the seeds.

5 Add the onion, chilli, tomatoes and coriander to the avocado. Season with black pepper and stir to mix.

6 Spoon the beans into a warmed serving dish or into four serving bowls. Serve with the tomato and avocado salsa and garnish with sprigs of fresh coriander.

PASTA AND PASTRY

Pasta or gnocchi makes a filling starch meal especially when combined with one of the different and original sauces included here. The sauces can also be served with brown rice or spooned over split baked potatoes or lightly steamed vegetables. While making pastry with wholewheat flour is recommended, it does no harm to your diet to occasionally use the ready-made, light and super-thin filo pastry, especially when it is filled with plenty of tasty Mediterranean vegetables or used to envelop a subtle combination of cream cheese, leeks and fresh herbs.

Chinese Primavera (S)

INGREDIENTS

Serves 4

350g/12oz capellini pasta (egg-free)
2.5ml/¹/₂ tsp salt
15ml/1 tbsp groundnut oil
1 red pepper, seeded
1 yellow pepper, seeded
115g/4oz/1 cup mangetouts
10 button mushrooms
3 spring onions
30ml/2 tbsp cornflour
15ml/1 tbsp olive oil
3 garlic cloves, finely chopped
175ml/6fl oz/³/₄ cup vegetable stock
45ml/3 tbsp dry sherry
30ml/2 tbsp sesame oil
15ml/1 tbsp light soy sauce
5ml/1 tsp chilli sauce
15ml/1 tbsp oyster sauce
2.5ml/¹/₂ tsp caster sugar
2.5ml/¹/₂ tsp Szechuan peppercorns,
   crushed
rind of 1 orange, cut into thin shreds,
   to garnish

1 Place the pasta in a large pan of boiling water with the salt and cook for 3 minutes. Drain in a colander and then transfer to a large bowl and stir in the groundnut oil.

--- COOK'S TIP ---

Capellini, vermicelli or angel hair pasta cooks very quickly and is ideal for quick meals. Serve with slices of fresh tomato sprinkled with chopped basil leaves and a little extra virgin olive oil.

2 Cut the peppers into matchsticks, halve the mangetouts, thinly slice the mushrooms and shred the spring onions. Stir them into the pasta.

3 Blend the cornflour with 30ml/ 2 tbsp water in a small bowl.

4 Heat the olive oil in a wok and stir-fry the garlic for 20 seconds. Add the vegetable stock, sherry, sesame oil, soy, chilli and oyster sauces, sugar and peppercorns. Bring to the boil and pour in the cornflour mixture, stirring all the time.

5 Add the pasta and vegetables and heat through for 2 minutes. Serve at once, garnished with orange rind.

Black Pasta with Raw Vegetables (S)

Black pasta derives its dramatic colour from the addition of squid ink. Alternatively you could use Japanese soba or buckwheat noodles, which have a nutty flavour and texture.

INGREDIENTS

Serves 4

3 garlic cloves, crushed
30ml/2 tbsp white tarragon vinegar
5ml/1 tsp Dijon mustard
90ml/6 tbsp extra virgin olive oil
5ml/1 tsp finely chopped fresh thyme
1 yellow pepper, seeded
1 red pepper, seeded
225g/8oz mangetouts, topped
  and tailed
6 radishes
4 ripe plum tomatoes, peeled
  and seeded
1 avocado
salt and freshly ground black pepper
275g/10oz black pasta (egg-free)
6 fresh basil leaves, to garnish

1 In a large bowl, blend together the garlic, vinegar, mustard, olive oil and chopped thyme. Season to taste with salt and pepper.

2 Cut the peppers into diamond shapes, halve the mangetouts and slice the radishes.

3 Dice the tomatoes. Peel, stone and slice the avocado. Place all the vegetables in a bowl and add the dressing, stirring thoroughly to mix.

4 Cook the pasta in plenty of slightly salted boiling water until *al dente*. The cooking time will vary depending on the type of pasta. Drain and tip into a large shallow serving dish. Cover with the vegetables and serve immediately, garnished with basil leaves.

Courgette and Dill Tart (S)

It is worth making your own pastry for this tart. Although shop-bought shortcrust pastry is a useful standby, it never tastes quite as good as home-made.

INGREDIENTS

Serves 4
115g/4oz/1 cup plain
    wholemeal flour
115g/4oz/1 cup self-raising flour
115g/4oz/8 tbsp unsalted butter,
    chilled and diced
75ml/5 tbsp ice-cold water
pinch salt

For the filling
15ml/1 tbsp sunflower oil
3 courgettes, thinly sliced
2 egg yolks
150ml/¼ pint/⅔ cup double cream
1 garlic clove, crushed
15ml/1 tbsp finely chopped fresh dill
salt and freshly ground black pepper

1 Sift the flours into a bowl, returning any of the wheat bran into the bowl, then place in a food processor. Add the salt and butter and process using the pulse button until the mixture resembles fine breadcrumbs.

2 Gradually add the water until the mixture forms a dough. Do not over process. Rest the pastry by wrapping it in clear cling film and placing in the fridge for 30 minutes.

3 Preheat the oven to 200°C/400°F/ Gas 6 and grease a 20cm/8in flan tin. Roll out the pastry and ease into the tin. Prick the base with a fork and bake "blind" for 10–15 minutes until lightly browned.

4 Meanwhile heat the oil in a frying pan and sauté the courgettes for 2–3 minutes until lightly browned, turning occasionally. Blend the egg yolks, double cream, garlic and dill in a small bowl. Season to taste with salt and pepper.

5 Line the pastry case with layers of courgette and gently pour over the cream mixture. Return to the oven for 25–30 minutes or until the filling is firm and lightly golden. Cool in the tin and then remove and serve.

Potato Gnocchi with Fresh Tomato Sauce (S)

Gnocchi make a substantial and tasty alternative to pasta. They are served with a fresh tomato sauce, which, because the tomatoes are simply warmed through for a short time, and not cooked, remains neutral.

INGREDIENTS

Serves 4

675g/1½lb potatoes, floury type
2 egg yolks
75g/3oz/¾ cup plain flour
salt
60ml/4 tbsp finely chopped fresh
  parsley, to garnish

For the sauce

450g/1lb plum tomatoes, peeled,
  seeded and chopped
30ml/2 tbsp melted butter

1 Preheat the oven to 200°C/400°F/ Gas 6. Scrub the potatoes and bake in their jackets in the oven for 1 hour or until the flesh feels soft when pricked with a fork.

2 Peel the potatoes while still warm, discarding the skins, and mash the flesh well. Add a little salt and stir in the egg yolks.

3 Place the potato mixture on a floured surface and knead in the flour to make a smooth elastic dough.

4 Shape the dough into small thumb-shapes by making long rolls and cutting them into segments. Press each gnocchi with the back of a fork to give a ridged effect. Place the gnocchi on a floured surface.

5 Cook the gnocchi in small batches in barely simmering, slightly salted water for about 10 minutes. Remove with a slotted spoon, drain well and keep warm.

6 To make the sauce, cook the tomatoes in the butter in a small pan for 1 minute. Sprinkle the gnocchi with chopped parsley and serve at once with the sauce.

Filo "Money Bags" with Creamy Leek Filling (S)

Ready-made fresh or frozen filo pastry is widely available in good supermarkets and can be used for both sweet and savoury dishes.

INGREDIENTS

Serves 4

115g/4oz/½ cup butter
225g/8oz/2 cups leeks, trimmed and
    finely chopped
225g/8oz/1 cup cream cheese
15ml/1 tbsp finely chopped fresh dill
15ml/1 tbsp finely chopped
    fresh parsley
2 spring onions, finely chopped
pinch of cayenne pepper
1 garlic clove, finely chopped
2.5ml/½ tsp salt
1.5ml/¼ tsp freshly ground
    black pepper
1 egg yolk
9 sheets filo pastry, thawed if frozen
lightly cooked leeks, to serve

1 Preheat the oven to 200°C/400°F/ Gas 6. Melt 25g/1oz/2 tbsp of the butter in a frying pan and fry the leeks for 4–5 minutes until soft. Drain off any liquid.

2 Put the cream cheese in a bowl and stir in the dill, parsley, spring onions, cayenne, garlic and seasoning. Add the egg yolk and leeks and stir well. Melt the remaining butter.

3 Place one sheet of filo pastry on a board, brush with a little of the melted butter and place another sheet on top. Brush again with butter and top with a third sheet of filo.

4 Cut the layered filo into four squares and place 20ml/1 rounded tbsp of the cheese mixture in the centre of each square. Gather up the edges into a "bag", twisting the top to seal.

5 Repeat with the other six sheets of filo to make 12 bags. Brush each bag with a little more butter.

6 Place the bags on a greased baking sheet and bake in the oven for 20–25 minutes until golden brown. Serve on a bed of lightly cooked leeks.

COOK'S TIP

For an attractive effect, tie each bag with a strip of blanched leek before serving.

Filo Baskets with Mediterranean Vegetables (S)

This richly flavoured vegetable filling may also be served with freshly cooked pasta or with jacket potatoes and soured cream.

INGREDIENTS

Makes about 30
1 small aubergine
8 sheets filo pastry, defrosted
115g/4oz/½ cup butter, melted
1 red pepper, seeded
1 yellow pepper, seeded
1 orange pepper, seeded
450g/1lb courgettes, topped and tailed
15ml/1 tbsp extra virgin olive oil
1 onion, finely chopped
2 garlic cloves, finely chopped
1 fresh thyme sprig
5ml/1 tsp sugar
5ml/1 tsp balsamic vinegar
salt and freshly ground black pepper
8 fresh basil leaves, shredded,
    to garnish

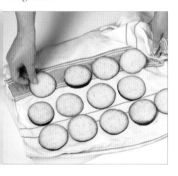

1 Preheat the oven to 180°C/350°F/ Gas 4. Slice the aubergine into thin rounds, place on a plate or board lined with a clean cloth and sprinkle with salt. Cover with the cloth and place a weighted plate on top. Leave for about 20 minutes to draw out the juices.

COOK'S TIP

Keep checking the filo baskets while they are baking as they brown very quickly and will become very brittle if overcooked.

2 Meanwhile, cut two sheets of filo pastry into 15 squares each and brush each square with melted butter. Arrange each square in a mini muffin tin. Repeat with the remaining filo, to form mini baskets, arranging the squares at angles to create a star effect. Keep the unused filo covered with a damp cloth as you work to prevent it drying out. Bake for 10 minutes until golden brown. Cool in the tins.

3 Cut the peppers into strips and slice the courgettes. Rinse the aubergine slices, pat dry and cut in half.

4 Heat the oil in a heavy-based saucepan and sauté the onion and garlic until soft but not brown. Add the peppers, courgettes, aubergine, thyme and sugar and cook over a low heat for 20 minutes, stirring occasionally. Stir in the balsamic vinegar and season with salt and pepper. Remove the sprig of thyme from the pan.

5 Remove the filo baskets from the muffin tins. Divide the vegetable mixture among the baskets and sprinkle each one with shredded basil leaves.

Pasta with Fresh Basil and Parsley Pesto (S)

Choose mixed plain, spinach and tomato pasta for this recipe, or, if you prefer, use one of the wholemeal varieties. The pesto may be made in advance and will keep for a few days in the fridge.

INGREDIENTS

Serves 4
400g/14oz mixed red, green and
  natural pasta shapes (egg-free)

For the pesto
2 garlic cloves, crushed
75g/3oz/¹⁄₂ cup pine nuts
50g/2oz/2 cups fresh basil leaves, plus
  extra to garnish
25g/1oz/¹⁄₂ cup fresh flat leaf parsley
150ml/¹⁄₄ pint/²⁄₃ cup extra virgin
  olive oil
salt and freshly ground black pepper

1 Cook the pasta in plenty of lightly salted boiling water until *al dente*. The cooking time will depend on the type of pasta shape you are using.

2 Meanwhile, place the garlic, pine nuts, basil and parsley in a blender or food processor and process for 30 seconds while gradually pouring in the oil, to make a thick sauce.

3 Drain the pasta and place on a large warmed serving plate. Pour over the pesto sauce and serve, garnished with extra basil.

— COOK'S TIP —

To vary the flavour of the pesto, use coriander instead of parsley.

Penne with Broccoli and Walnut Sauce (S)

This Italian sauce is truly delicious. It is traditionally served with pasta but can also be spread thickly on slices of fresh or grilled ciabatta bread and served with chunks of celery, tomatoes, cucumber and radishes.

INGREDIENTS

Serves 4
275g/10oz dried penne (egg-free)
450g/1lb fresh broccoli, cut into
  equal-size florets

For the sauce
50g/2oz/¹⁄₂ cup walnuts
30ml/2 tbsp fresh brown breadcrumbs
75g/3oz/1¹⁄₂ cups fresh parsley
120ml/4fl oz/¹⁄₂ cup extra virgin
  olive oil
30ml/2 tbsp single cream
salt and freshly ground black pepper

1 First make the sauce. Place the walnuts, breadcrumbs and parsley in a blender or food processor and process for 20 seconds. With the machine running, gradually add the olive oil to make a slightly textured paste. Add the cream and seasoning.

2 Cook the pasta in plenty of boiling salted water for 12–15 minutes until *al dente*.

3 Steam the broccoli florets for about 3 minutes until they are tender but still with a little crunch.

4 Drain the pasta, place in a bowl and mix with the broccoli. Spoon on to individual serving plates and pour the sauce over.

CAKES, BAKES AND BISCUITS

*Home-made cakes are far better than
shop-bought and prepared with
naturally sweet fruits, such as dates and
bananas, they are healthier, too, since
they need little extra sweetening.
Simple breads, such as focaccia, are easy
to make at home and worth trying.
Cheese and biscuits are a classic way of
finishing a meal and it is a joy to
discover that Sunflower and Almond
Sesame Crackers, which are a neutral
food, can be combined with any cheese,
while Sweet Almond Biscuits contain
only a little sugar and make the ideal
partner for ice cream or yogurt.*

Walnut Bread (S)

Just the smell of freshly baked bread is appetizing and lingers for hours afterwards. This loaf will disappear very quickly and it is wise to make several and put one in the freezer. Serve warm with soups or salad for a light lunch.

INGREDIENTS

Makes 1 loaf
150g/5oz/1¼ cups rye flour
150g/5oz/1¼ cups strong white
  bread flour
5ml/1 tsp easy-blend dried yeast
2.5ml/½ tsp salt
15g/½oz/1 tbsp butter, softened
5ml/1 tsp honey
115g/4oz/1 cup walnuts, halved
sunflower oil, for greasing

1 Butter a 450g/1lb loaf tin and sift the flours into a bowl. Stir in the yeast and salt.

2 Add the butter and honey, then add 150ml/¼ pint/⅔ cup warm water and mix to a soft dough.

3 Turn the dough on to a floured surface and knead lightly to make a ball. Place in a lightly oiled bowl and cover the dough with oiled clear film. Set aside to rise in a warm place for about 2 hours.

4 Turn the dough out on to a floured surface and knock back. Scatter the walnuts over the dough and knead lightly until the walnuts are evenly worked into the dough.

5 Shape the dough into an oblong and place in the tin. Cover with a damp cloth and leave to rise for about 1 hour until doubled in size. Preheat the oven to 240°C/475°F/Gas 9.

6 Lightly spray the loaf with water, then bake for 15 minutes. Reduce the oven temperature to 200°C/400°F/ Gas 6 and bake for 30 minutes more. To check that the bread is cooked, remove from the tin and tap the bottom; it should sound hollow. If it does not, return the loaf to the oven for a further 5 minutes, then test again. Turn out of the tin and leave to cool completely on a wire rack.

Oat and Raisin Drop Scones (S)

Serve these scones at tea time or as a dessert with real maple syrup or organic honey. If you are feeling indulgent, add a dollop of soured cream or crème fraîche.

INGREDIENTS

Makes about 16

75g/3oz/³/₄ cup self-raising flour
2.5ml/¹/₂ tsp baking powder
50g/2oz/¹/₂ cup raisins
25g/1oz/¹/₄ cup fine oatmeal
25g/1oz/¹/₄ cup caster sugar
grated rind of 1 orange
2 egg yolks
10g/¹/₄oz/¹/₂ tbsp unsalted butter, melted
200ml/7fl oz/³/₄ cup single cream
200ml/7fl oz/³/₄ cup water
pinch of salt

1 Sift together the flour, salt and baking powder.

2 Add the raisins, oatmeal, sugar and orange rind. Gradually beat in the egg yolks, butter, cream and water to make a creamy batter.

3 Lightly grease and heat a large frying pan or griddle and drop about 30ml/2 tbsp of batter at a time on to the pan or griddle to make six or seven small pancakes.

4 Cook over a moderate heat until bubbles show on the scones' surface, then turn them over and cook for a further 2 minutes until golden.

5 Transfer the scones to a plate and keep warm while cooking the remaining mixture. Serve warm.

Banana Cake (S)

INGREDIENTS

Makes 1 cake
90g/3½oz/¾ cup plain flour
2.5ml/½ tsp ground cinnamon
5ml/1 tsp baking powder
75g/3oz/⅔ cup sultanas
50g/2oz/½ cup roughly
  chopped walnuts
90g/3½oz/½ cup caster sugar
50g/2oz/4 tbsp unsalted butter,
  softened
2 large ripe bananas, peeled
  and mashed
2 egg yolks
30ml/2 tbsp whisky (optional)

--- VARIATION ---

If preferred, use two or three drops of
vanilla essence instead of the whisky.

1 Preheat the oven to 190°C/375°F/
Gas 5. Lightly butter a 450g/1lb
loaf tin and line with greaseproof paper.

2 Sift the flour, cinnamon and baking
powder into a bowl, add the
sultanas and walnuts and mix well.

3 In another bowl, cream the sugar
and butter together until light and
fluffy, then beat in the bananas, egg
yolks and whisky, if using. Fold in the
dry ingredients.

4 Pour the mixture into the prepared
loaf tin and cook for 55 minutes or
until a skewer inserted into the centre
comes out clean. Leave to cool in the
tin before turning out.

Date and Honey Bars (S)

Fresh dates, such as Deglet Noor
and Medjool, are a good source
of natural fibre, yet are kind and
gentle on the digestive system.
For a slightly different, more
toffee flavour, replace the honey
with real maple syrup.

INGREDIENTS

Makes 16
175g/6oz/1 cup fresh dates, stoned and
  roughly chopped
45ml/3 tbsp honey
30ml/2 tbsp lemon juice
150g/5oz/1¼ cups plain flour
150ml/¼ pint/⅔ cup water
1.5ml/¼ tsp freshly grated nutmeg
115g/4oz/1 cup self-raising flour, sifted
25g/1oz/2 tbsp brown sugar
150g/5oz/1¼ cups rolled oats
175g/6oz/¾ cup unsalted
  butter, melted

1 Preheat the oven to 190°C/375°F/
Gas 5. Butter the base of an
18cm/7in square cake tin and line with
greaseproof paper.

2 Place the dates, honey, lemon juice,
plain flour and water in a heavy-
based pan. Bring slowly to the boil,
stirring all the time. Remove from the
heat and leave to cool.

3 Mix together the nutmeg, self-
raising flour, sugar, oats and melted
butter and spread half of the mixture
over the base of the cake tin, pressing
down well.

4 Spread the date mixture over the
top and finish with the remaining
oat mixture, pressing evenly all over the
surface with the back of a spoon. Bake
for about 25 minutes until golden.
Cool in the cake tin for 1 hour, then
cut into bars.

Focaccia (S)

This simple-to-make Italian bread is similar to pizza and needs a really fine extra virgin olive oil to give it its robust taste. Serve it warm with home-made vegetable soup.

INGREDIENTS

Makes 1 loaf
350g/12oz/3 cups plain flour
2.5ml/½ tsp fine salt
10ml/2 tsp easy-blend dried yeast
175ml/6fl oz/¾ cup warm water
45ml/3 tbsp extra virgin olive oil
1 fresh rosemary or sage sprig,
    coarsely chopped
5ml/1 tsp coarse salt

VARIATION

As an alternative, instead of rosemary, top the bread with chopped black olives and sliced red onion.

1 Place the flour and fine salt in a bowl, sprinkle on the yeast and mix well. Pour in the warm water and 30ml/2 tbsp of the olive oil and work in with your hands to make a soft dough. Add a little more water if necessary. Turn out the dough on to a floured surface and knead well for about 10 minutes until it is smooth, soft and elastic.

2 Place the dough in a bowl, oiled with a little of the remaining olive oil, cover with clear film and leave in a warm place for about 1½ hours until doubled in size.

3 Punch the dough down, knead again for 1 minute, then place on an oiled baking sheet. Pat it out to a thickness of about 2cm/¾in. Press your fingers into the dough to make indentations all over. Brush the top with the remaining olive oil and sprinkle with the rosemary or sage leaves and coarse salt. Cover with a damp cloth and leave to rise for about 30 minutes.

4 Meanwhile, preheat the oven to 220°C/425°F/Gas 7. When the focaccia has risen, bake for about 25 minutes until golden brown.

Flat Breads with Fresh Sage (S)

These savoury flat breads are easy to make and need no proving or special equipment. They are delicious served with home-made vegetable soups, vegetable purées, hummus or a crisp raw vegetable salad.

INGREDIENTS

Makes 12
225g/8oz/2 cups plain flour
225g/8oz/2 cups wholemeal flour
2.5ml/½ tsp salt
20 fresh sage leaves, finely chopped
325ml/10fl oz/1⅓ cups water
about 10ml/2 tsp sunflower oil,
    for frying

1 Sift the flours and salt together into a large bowl. Add the sage and slowly add the water while mixing to make a soft dough. Knead for 10 minutes on a floured surface until the dough is smooth and elastic. Cover and rest for 30 minutes.

2 Divide the dough into 12 balls. Place each one on a floured surface and flatten to make little rounds. Prick each round with a fork. Heat a little oil in a heavy-based frying pan and fry the breads for 1–2 minutes on each side until slightly browned and crisp. Serve hot.

Sweet Almond Biscuits (N)

Serve these crisp biscuits with ice cream or fruit fool, or more simply with fresh fruit salad, yogurt or a spoonful of thick cream. Make a batch in advance and keep them in an airtight tin.

INGREDIENTS

Makes about 24
30ml/2 tbsp milk
1 egg yolk
225g/8oz/2 cups ground almonds, plus extra for rolling out
25g/1oz/2 tbsp caster sugar
5ml/1 tsp baking powder
25g/1oz/2 tbsp butter, melted
2.5ml/½ tsp vanilla essence

VARIATION

The egg yolk is not essential but helps to bind the mixture together. If preferred, use an extra 15ml/1 tbsp milk.

1 Preheat the oven to 190°C/375°F/ Gas 5 and blend together the milk and egg yolk.

2 Mix the ground almonds, sugar and baking powder in a bowl and stir in the butter, vanilla essence and milk-and-egg mixture.

3 Work the mixture with your hands to form a moist dough and then roll out to about 5mm/¼in thickness on a cool surface lightly dusted with extra ground almonds.

4 Cut the dough into rounds using a 6cm/2½in pastry cutter.

5 Transfer the dough rounds to a non-stick baking sheet and bake for about 10 minutes until lightly browned. Cool on a wire rack.

Sunflower and Almond Sesame Crackers (N)

One thing food combiners often yearn for is cheese and biscuits at the end of a meal. These neutral crackers can be served either with your favourite cheese or as a base for fish or meat canapés.

INGREDIENTS

Makes about 24

130g/4½oz/1 cup ground sunflower seeds
90g/3½oz/¾ cup ground almonds
5ml/1 tsp baking powder
30ml/2 tbsp milk
1 egg yolk
25g/1oz/2 tbsp butter, melted
25g/1oz/¼ cup sesame seeds

1 Preheat the oven to 190°C/375°F/ Gas 5. Reserve 25g/1oz/¼ cup of the ground sunflower seeds for rolling out, and mix the remaining ground seeds with the ground almonds and baking powder in a bowl.

2 Blend together the milk and egg yolk and stir into the ground seed and almond mixture with the melted butter, mixing well. Gently work the mixture with your hands to form a moist dough.

VARIATION

Sprinkle some poppy seeds on top of a few of the biscuits before baking.

3 Roll out the dough to about 5mm/¼in thickness on a cool surface, lightly dusted with a little of the reserved ground sunflower seeds, with a little more sprinkled on top to prevent sticking.

4 Sprinkle the dough with sesame seeds and cut into rounds using a 5cm/2in pastry cutter. Lift on to a non-stick baking sheet.

5 Bake the crackers for about 10 minutes until lightly browned. Cool on a wire rack.

DESSERTS

Desserts don't have to be wicked to be wonderful and a small indulgence does no harm, particularly when it is made from the very best ingredients. When you are planning a menu, remember to match protein desserts with protein main courses and starch desserts with starch main courses. All the recipes are simple to make, and desserts such as Stem Ginger Ice Cream, Passion Fruit Brûlée and Soft Fruit Pavlova are perfect for entertaining, while Pear and Cardamom Sponge will appeal to everyone and could be served at any family celebration.

Sweet Pear and Cardamom Sponge (S)

Choose very sweet dessert pears, like Comice or Williams, for this delicious dessert. They need to be completely ripe and very juicy. Serve with a dollop of whipped cream or ice cream.

INGREDIENTS

Serves 4

5 pears
10 green cardamom pods
115g/4oz/1 cup self-raising flour
5ml/1 tsp baking powder
115g/4oz/generous ½ cup caster sugar
115g/4oz/½ cup butter, softened
3 egg yolks
30–45ml/2–3 tbsp warm water

1 Preheat the oven to 190°C/375°F/ Gas 5. Line the base of a 20cm/8in diameter cake tin with greaseproof paper and then butter and lightly flour the sides.

2 Peel the pears, cut them in half and remove the cores. Lay the fruit cut side up in a circle in the bottom of the prepared tin.

3 Remove the cardamom seeds from the pods and crush the seeds lightly using a pestle and mortar.

4 Sift together the flour and baking powder. Add the sugar, crushed cardamom seeds, butter, egg yolks and 30ml/2 tbsp of the water. Beat with an electric or hand whisk until creamy. The mixture should fall off a spoon; if it does not, add a little more water.

5 Place the mixture on top of the pears and level with a knife. Bake for 45–50 minutes until the cake is firm.

6 Turn the cake out on to a wire rack and peel off the greaseproof paper. Cool before serving.

Stem Ginger Ice Cream (N)

This rich and flavourful ice cream goes beautifully with sliced fresh pears and bananas at the end of a starch meal or with gooseberry and apple purée after a protein main course.

INGREDIENTS

Serves 4

15ml/1 tbsp clear honey
4 egg yolks
600ml/1 pint/2½ cups double cream, lightly whipped
4 pieces of preserved stem ginger, chopped into tiny dice

1 Place the honey and 150ml/¼ pint/ ⅔ cup water in a small saucepan and heat until the honey is completely dissolved. Remove from the heat and allow to cool.

2 Place the egg yolks in a large bowl and whisk gently until pale and frothy. Slowly add the honey syrup and fold in the whipped cream.

3 Pour the mixture into a plastic freezer container and freeze for about 45 minutes or until the ice cream is freezing at the edges.

—— COOK'S TIP ——

Transfer the ice cream from the freezer to the fridge 20 minutes before serving.

4 Transfer to a bowl and whisk again. Mix in the stem ginger, reserving a few pieces for decoration. Freeze again for 2–4 hours. Serve the ice cream in scoops, decorated with the reserved stem ginger.

Passion Fruit Brûlée (P)

Fruit brûlées are usually made with double cream, but thick yogurt, which has a rich flavour and is more easily digested, works equally well. The brown sugar required for this recipe is reserved for the crunchy caramelized topping as the passion fruit pulp is naturally very sweet.

INGREDIENTS

Serves 4
4 passion fruit
300ml/½ pint/1¼ cups Greek or thick natural yogurt
75g/3oz/½ cup soft light brown sugar

1 Cut the passion fruit in half using a very sharp knife. Use a teaspoon to scoop out all the pulp and seeds and divide equally between four small ovenproof ramekins.

2 Spoon equal amounts of the yogurt on top of the fruit and smooth the surface until it is completely flat and level. Chill for at least 2 hours.

3 Place the sugar in a small saucepan with 15ml/1 tbsp water and heat gently until the sugar has melted and caramelized. Pour over the yogurt: the caramel will harden within 1 minute. Keep the brûlées in a cool place until ready to serve.

Grilled Nectarines with Amaretto (P)

Amaretto, the sweet almond-flavoured liqueur from Italy, adds a touch of luxury to many soft fruits, particularly peaches and nectarines. Enhance the nutty taste by scattering some lightly toasted flaked almonds, still hot from the grill, on top of the crème fraîche just before serving.

INGREDIENTS

Serves 4
6 ripe nectarines
30ml/2 tbsp clear honey
60ml/4 tbsp Amaretto
crème fraîche, to serve

1 Cut the nectarines in half by running a small sharp knife down the side of each fruit from top to bottom, pushing the knife right through to the stone. Gently ease the nectarine apart and remove the stone.

2 Place the nectarines cut side up in an ovenproof dish and drizzle about 2.5ml/½ tsp honey and 5ml/1 tsp Amaretto over each half.

3 Preheat the grill until very hot and then grill the fruit for a few minutes until slightly charred. Arrange the nectarine halves on four small serving plates and serve with a little crème fraîche.

Honey Almond Cream (N)

This dessert is best served after a light main course as it is very rich and deliciously indulgent. Serve with seasonal soft berries such as blueberries, raspberries or blackberries after a protein meal. Alternatively serve with slices of very sweet fresh pears or bananas after a starch main course.

INGREDIENTS

Serves 4

275g/10oz/1¼ cups cream cheese or mascarpone
50g/2oz/½ cup ground almonds
1 egg yolk
15ml/1 tbsp clear honey
tiny drop of vanilla essence
50ml/2fl oz/¼ cup double cream
fresh fruit, to serve

1 Line a 10cm/4in new or well-scrubbed terracotta flowerpot with fine muslin, allowing a generous overhang around the sides.

2 Blend together the cheese and ground almonds in a bowl.

VARIATION

A small handful of sultanas or raisins can be added to the cheese mixture, if liked.

3 Beat the egg yolk and honey together in another bowl and add the vanilla essence.

4 Lightly whip the cream, fold it into the cheese mixture and stir carefully until the mixture has the consistency of thick mayonnaise. Add the egg and honey and mix gently.

5 Spoon into the flower pot and fold over the muslin to cover. Place a small weighted plate on the top.

6 Stand the flowerpot in a dish to catch any excess liquid and place in the fridge overnight. When ready to serve, carefully turn out on to a plate and serve with the fresh fruit.

Soft Fruit Pavlova (P)

There is a lot of sugar in meringue, but for special occasions this is the queen of desserts and a practical way of using up egg whites left over after making ice cream or mayonnaise.

INGREDIENTS

Serves 4

4 egg whites
175g/6oz/1¼ cups caster sugar
30ml/2 tbsp redcurrant jelly
300ml/½ pint/1¼ cups double cream, whipped, or crème fraîche
15ml/1 tbsp rose water
450g/1lb mixed soft fruits, such as blackberries, blueberries, redcurrants, raspberries or loganberries
10ml/2 tsp sifted icing sugar
pinch of salt

1 Preheat the oven to 140°C/275°F/ Gas 1. Oil a baking sheet. Whisk the egg whites with a pinch of salt in a spotlessly clean bowl, until they are white and stiff. Slowly add the sugar and keep whisking until the mixture makes stiff, glossy peaks.

--- COOK'S TIP ---

Meringues may be made in advance and stored in an airtight tin or better still kept in the freezer.

2 Spoon the meringue into a 25cm/10in round on the baking sheet, making a slight indentation in the centre and soft crests around the outside. Bake for 1–1½ hours until the meringue is firm. Keep checking as the meringue can easily overcook and turn brown. Transfer the meringue to a serving plate.

3 Melt the redcurrant jelly in a small bowl resting in a pan of hot water. Cool slightly, then spread the jelly in the centre of the meringue.

4 Gently mix the rose water with the whipped cream or crème fraîche and spoon into the centre of the meringue. Arrange the fruits on top and dust lightly with icing sugar.

Papaya and Green Grapes with Mint Syrup (S)

Papaya is rich in vitamins A, C
and E and also contains calcium,
phosphorus and iron. It is very
easily digested and has a tonic
effect on the stomach, so makes
the perfect dessert to follow a
richly flavoured starch course,
such as Filo Baskets with
Mediterranean Vegetables.

INGREDIENTS

Serves 4
2 large papaya
225g/8oz seedless green grapes
juice of 3 limes
2.5cm/1in fresh root ginger, peeled
 and finely grated
15ml/1 tbsp clear honey
5 fresh mint leaves, cut into thin strips,
 plus extra whole leaves, to decorate

1 Peel the papaya and cut into small
cubes, discarding the seeds. Cut the
grapes in half.

2 In a bowl, mix together the lime
juice, ginger, honey and shredded
mint leaves.

3 Add the papaya and grapes and toss
well. Leave in a cool place to
marinate for 1 hour.

4 Serve in a large dish or individual
stemmed glasses, garnished with
whole fresh mint leaves.

Orange Granita with Strawberries (P)

Granita is a crunchy sorbet that
is simple to make and requires no
special equipment. Use very
juicy oranges and really ripe
strawberries that do not need
any additional sweetening.

INGREDIENTS

Serves 4
6 large juicy oranges
350g/12oz ripe strawberries
finely pared strips of orange rind,
 to decorate

COOK'S TIP

Granita will keep for up to 3 weeks in the
freezer. Sweet pink grapefruits or deep red
blood oranges can be used for a different
flavour and colour. Add a little fresh lemon
juice if you prefer a more tart ice.

1 Squeeze the juice from the oranges
and pour into a shallow freezer-
proof bowl.

2 Place the bowl in the freezer.
Remove after 30 minutes and beat
the semi-frozen juice thoroughly with a
wooden spoon. Repeat this process at
30-minute intervals over a 4-hour
period. This will break the ice crystals
down into small particles. Halve the
strawberries and arrange them on a
serving plate. Scoop the granita into
serving glasses, decorate with strips of
orange rind and serve immediately with
the strawberries.

INDEX

Acid-forming foods, 6
Alkaline-forming foods, 6
Almonds: honey almond cream, 92
  sunflower and almond sesame
    crackers, 85
  sweet almond biscuits, 84
Almost-dry roasted vegetables, 47
Amaretto, grilled nectarines with, 90
Anchovies: anchovy and parsley
    relish, 16
  grilled monkfish with home-made
    tapenade, 36
Apples: feta and apple salad, 52
  pheasant breasts with caramelized
    apples, 25
Aubergine and spinach terrines, 51
Avocados: bean feast with tomato and
    avocado salsa, 65
  soured cream and avocado dipping
    sauce, 12

Banana cake, 80
Basil and parsley pesto, pasta with, 74
Beans: bean feast with tomato and
    avocado salsa, 65
  sprouting, 9
Biscuits: sunflower and almond sesame
    crackers, 85
  sweet almond biscuits, 84
Bread: flat breads with fresh sage, 82
  focaccia, 82
  walnut bread, 78
Broccoli, penne with walnut sauce
    and, 74
Butterflied Mediterranean prawns, 40

Cabbage: fennel and chervil coleslaw, 55
  Savoy cabbage and vegetable pie, 61
Cakes: banana cake, 80
  date and honey bars, 80
Carbohydrates, 6, 7, 9
Carrots: celeriac, turnip and carrot
    purée, 48
Celeriac, turnip and carrot purée, 48
Cheese: feta and apple salad, 52
Cheese, soft: filo "money bags" with
    creamy leek filling, 72
  honey almond cream, 92
Chick-peas: falafels with tahini
    dressing, 58
  hummus with baked vegetable
    chips, 59
Chicken: chicken and coconut curry, 28
  grilled spiced chicken, 26
  poached chicken with mustard
    mayonnaise, 29
  stir-fried chicken with lime and
    ginger, 30
Chinese primavera, 68
Cod: roasted cod with fresh tomato
    sauce, 34
Coleslaw, fennel and herb, 55
Coriander: fresh coriander and yogurt
    dipping sauce, 14

Courgette and dill tart, 70
Cracked wheat salad with walnuts and
    herbs, 60
Crackers, sunflower and almond
    sesame, 85
Cucumber: salmon with yogurt and mint
    dressing, 39
Curry, chicken and coconut, 28
Date and honey bars, 80
Desserts, 86–94
Duck: crispy duck breast with pak
    choi, 30
Falafels with tahini dressing, 58
Fats, 9
Fennel: fennel and herb coleslaw, 55
  mussels in fennel and white wine, 42
Feta and apple salad, 52
Filo baskets with Mediterranean
    vegetables, 73
Filo "money bags" with creamy leek
    filling, 72
Fish and seafood, 33–43
  fish stock, 9
  Thai fish soup, 20
Flat breads with fresh sage, 82
Focaccia, 82
Food classification, 6
Fruit, 6, 8
  soft fruit pavlova, 93

Gazpacho salsa, 16
Ginger: stem ginger ice cream, 89
  stir-fried green beans with, 48
Gnocchi: potato gnocchi with fresh
    tomato sauce, 71
Granita: orange granita with
    strawberries, 94
Grapes: papaya and green grapes with
    mint syrup, 94
Green beans: stir-fried green beans with
    ginger, 48

Haddock in spinach parcels with pepper
    purée, 35
Hay system, 6
Herbs, 8
  mixed green leaf and herb salad, 52
Honey almond cream, 92
Hummus with baked vegetable chips, 59

Ice cream, stem ginger, 89
Ingredients, 8–9
Italian rocket and potato soup, 18

Kebabs, Moroccan lamb, 26

Lamb kebabs, Moroccan, 26
Leeks: filo "money bags" with creamy
    leek filling, 72
Lentil risotto with vegetables, 64

Mayonnaise: fresh mayonnaise, 14
  poached chicken with mustard
    mayonnaise, 29
Meringues: soft fruit pavlova, 93
"Money bags" with creamy leek
    filling, 72
Monkfish: fried monkfish with home-
    made tapenade, 36
Moroccan lamb kebabs, 26
Mushrooms: stoved mixed
    mushrooms, 50
  wild rice and grain pilaf with
    mushrooms, 62
Mussels in fennel and white wine, 42

Nectarines: grilled nectarines with
    Amaretto, 90
Neutral foods, 7

Oat and raisin drop scones, 79
Oils, 9
Olives: grilled monkfish with home-
    made tapenade, 36
Orange granita with strawberries, 94
Oriental salad, 54

Pak choi, crispy duck breast with, 30
Papaya and green grapes with mint
    syrup, 94
Parsley: anchovy and parsley relish, 16
Passion fruit brûlée, 90
Pasta: black pasta with raw vegetable s, 69
  Chinese primavera, 68
  pasta with fresh basil and parsley
    pesto, 74
  penne with broccoli and walnut sauce, 74
Pavlova, soft fruit, 93
Pears: sweet pear and cardamom
    sponge, 88
Penne with broccoli and walnut sauce, 74
Peppers: cream of grilled pepper soup, 19
  haddock in spinach parcels with
    pepper purée, 35
  pork fillet with red pepper and pine
    nuts, 24
Pesto: pasta with fresh basil and parsley
    pesto, 74
Pheasant breasts with caramelized
    apples, 25
Pilaf: wild rice and grain pilaf with
    mushrooms, 62
Pine nuts: pasta with fresh basil and
    parsley pesto, 74
  pork fillet with red pepper and pine
    nuts, 24
  Polenta, grilled, 62
Pork fillet with red pepper and pine
    nuts, 24
Potatoes: Italian rocket and potato
    soup, 18
  potato gnocchi with fresh tomato
    sauce, 71
Prawns, butterflied Mediterranean, 40
Protein foods, 6, 7, 8

Rice: lentil risotto with vegetables, 64
  wild rice and grain pilaf with
    mushrooms, 62
Rocket: Italian rocket and potato
    soup, 18

Salads, 8
  cracked wheat salad with walnuts and
    fresh herbs, 60
  fennel and chervil coleslaw, 55
  feta and apple salad, 52
  mixed green leaf and herb salad, 52
  oriental salad, 54
  vegetable salad with tahini tofu
    dressing, 12
Salmon with yogurt and mint
    dressing, 39
Salsas: gazpacho, 16
  tomato and avocado, 65
Sardines: stuffed sardines with fresh
    rosemary, 36
Sauces: fresh coriander and yogurt
    dipping sauce, 14
  soured cream and avocado dipping
    sauce, 12

Savoy cabbage and vegetable pie, 61
Scallops: seared scallops with lemon and
    thyme, 40
Scones, oat and raisin drop, 79
Sea bass en papillote, whole, 38
Seafarer's stew, 43
Seafood and fish, 32–43
Smoked haddock: seafarer's stew, 43
Soups: cream of grilled pepper soup, 19
  Italian rocket and potato soup, 18
  star-gazer vegetable soup, 21
  Thai fish soup, 20
Soured cream and avocado dipping
    sauce, 12
Spices, 8
Spinach: aubergine and spinach
    terrines, 51
  haddock in spinach parcels with
    pepper purée, 35
Sprouting beans, 9
  feta and apple salad, 52
Star-gazer vegetable soup, 21
Starch foods, 6, 7, 9
Stock: fish, 9
  vegetable, 9
Stoved mixed mushrooms, 50
Strawberries, orange granita with, 94
Sunflower and almond sesame
    crackers, 85
Sweet almond biscuits, 84
Sweet pear and cardamom sponge, 88
Sweeteners, 9

Tahini dressing, falafels with, 58
Tapenade, grilled monkfish with, 36
Tart, courgette and dill, 70
Terrines, aubergine and spinach, 51
Thai fish soup, 20
Tofu: vegetable salad with tahini tofu
    dressing, 12
Tomatoes: bean feast with tomato and
    avocado salsa, 65
  gazpacho salsa, 16
  potato gnocchi with fresh tomato
    sauce, 71
  roasted cod with fresh tomato
    sauce, 34
Turnips: celeriac, turnip and carrot
    purée, 48

Vegetables, 6, 8, 44–45
  almost-dry roasted vegetables, 47
  black pasta with raw vegetables, 69
  Chinese primavera, 68
  filo baskets with Mediterranean
    vegetables, 73
  hummus with baked vegetable
    chips, 59
  Savoy cabbage and vegetable pie, 61
  star-gazer vegetable soup, 21
  vegetable stock, 9
  winter vegetable ragout, 46

Walnut bread, 78
Wheat berries: wild rice and grain pilaf
    with mushrooms, 62
Wild rice and grain pilaf with
    mushrooms, 62
Winter vegetable ragout, 46